The Military-Industrial Firm

John Francis Gorgol
prepared for publication by
Ira Kleinfeld
foreword by
Seymour Melman

The Praeger Special Studies program—
utilizing the most modern and efficient book
production techniques and a selective
worldwide distribution network—makes
available to the academic, government, and
business communities significant, timely
research in U.S. and international economic, social, and political development.

The Military-Industrial Firm
A Practical Theory and Model

PRAEGER SPECIAL STUDIES IN U.S. ECONOMIC AND SOCIAL DEVELOPMENT

Praeger Publishers   New York   Washington   London

PRAEGER PUBLISHERS
111 Fourth Avenue, New York, N.Y. 10003, U.S.A.
5, Cromwell Place, London S.W.7, England

Published in the United States of America in 1972
by Praeger Publishers, Inc.

Library of Congress Catalog Card Number: 75-170024

Printed in the United States of America

For 20,000 industrial enterprises in the United States, the classic model of the autonomous, cost-minimizing, profit-maximizing industrial firm is not a competent base for explaining the pattern of operations. These 20,000 enterprises are those engaged in producing for the Department of Defense. They range in size from industrial giants like Lockheed Aircraft Corporation and General Electric Company to smaller enterprises employing tens of employees. The larger firms are prime contractors, and many smaller firms are subcontractors to the Department of Defense.

Firms like Lockheed are overwhelmingly engaged in work on behalf of the Pentagon, while the General Electric Company has had about 25 percent of its net sales oriented to the Department of Defense. In the former enterprise, the characteristics of the military-industrial firm dominate the scene. In the case of the multidivision firm, like General Electric, it is the military-serving divisions that take on the special characteristics of the military-industrial firm, rather than the enterprise as a whole.

In the classic theory of industrial capitalism, the enterprise is characteristically autonomous. That means that the management (entrepreneur) is the final decision-maker with respect to what shall be produced, the quantity, how to produce, the price, and distribution of the product. Moreover, the pressures of market competition compel, to greater or lesser degree, efforts to minimize costs on behalf of profit accumulation, which, in turn, is the basis for further investment by the private-industrial management.

These characteristic conditions are substantially modified in the military-industrial enterprise. For there, the autonomy of the local management is limited

by the decisions that are made by the central management located in the Pentagon. Owing to the nature
of the production situation, especially the characteristics of military products, "competence" to meet
the requirements of the Pentagon has characteristically been given greater importance than cost-
minimizing strategies. Finally, in place of the
profit-maximizing strategies of the autonomous industrial managements, the military-industrial firm
operates to maintain and enlarge its decision power
through a set of strategies that are more in the
nature of "subsidy-maximizing" rather than profit-
maximizing.

The importance of this book for industrial
economics is that it outlines the characteristics of
an enterprise that, by 1971, is at the center of
the American industrial system, with preferred access
to capital and guarantees of sustained operation
through the allocation of public funds in the name
of defense. I find it hard to conceive of a competent theory of American industrial capitalism in
the second half of this century that does not take
into account the new characteristics of the military-
industrial enterprise.

The theory of the military-industrial firm, as
developed by John Gorgol, opens up a host of issues
including the problem: What is the relative decision
power of the military-industrial enterprise as compared to the state management on behalf of which the
enterprise is operated? For understanding the autonomous industrial firm, most economists and others as-
sume that final decision authority is in the hands
of the firm's management, even where government is
an important customer. In the case of the military-
industrial firm, this ordinary understanding must be
reexamined.

In no conceivable case may the military-industrial firm initiate production of military products
of its choice and sell them to customers of its
choice. The production of weapons systems is not
undertaken except by order of the Pentagon's state
management, which has final decision authority in

this respect. Indeed, the network of regulations and the system of administrative controls operated by the Pentagon's state management extends to every major area of managerial decision-making (see S. Melman, Pentagon Capitalism, McGraw Hill, 1970, Chapter 2). This is not to say that the managements of particular military-industry enterprises do not compete against each other, aggressively, for securing shares of the orders and the capital funds available from the controlling state management. (They also join politically to back military budgets, etc.) It is to say, however, that it is the state management, operating in the fashion of a central administrative office, that makes final decisions in these matters. Thus, however much a particular military-industrial firm tries to affect top-management decisions--by political influence of former military officers, congressmen, local mayors, trade union officers, etc.--it is the top management in the Department of Defense that makes the final decisions on allocation of new capital funds and on allocation of military work.

The consequences for the macroeconomy of the United States are far-ranging, owing to the operation of this vast network of military-industrial enter- prises. Not the least of these effects is the fact that these organizations, as organized entities, are rarely transferable to civilian work; if at all, then only with great difficulty. As a result of this condition, there is a high degree of dependency on military-industry employment that is concentrated in the United States by industry, by profession and by locality. These concentrations of military-industry work and their effects on regional economies give special importance to the understanding of the unique characteristics of the military-industrial enterprise as developed by John Gorgol.

Finally, may I call attention to the appendix material, which, by brief comparison of the military- industrial firm with the Soveit enterprise, opens up a fascinating set of problems for students of economic institutions and their development.

With sorrow, I record the untimely death of John
Francis Gorgol. That explains the requirement for
the intervention of other persons to prepare this
volume for present publication. We are grateful to
Ira Kleinfeld for his careful and conscientious
editing of the original Gorgol manuscript.

Seymour Melman
Professor of Industrial
   Engineering
Columbia University

This book is an attempt to formulate a theory and model that are capable of giving a credible explanation of the behavior of what has become an important production entity in the American economy: the military-supplying firm. Such an innovation implies an abandonment of currently recognized economic theories as they relate to the miliatry firm. But in times when the latter has taken on such great importance in the national life, a new view is precisely what is needed. This is necessitated by the very poor formal understanding we have of such a firm's operation. Proof lies in the confusion and mistrust of defense firms resulting from the recent highly publicized difficulties of these companies, the case of Lockheed Aircraft Corporation being the most controversial. Not only have these firms come under close public scrutiny (even if at a superficial level) but a heated national debate has accompanied this scrutiny as well.

It is important to understand the actions of these firms not only because of what they produce but because they are large employers. Many Americans owe their livelihoods and, thus, some allegiance to the activity of military firms. At the same time, however, military research and development drains a significant fraction of the nation's technical and scientific manpower, leaving other activities requiring productive research endeavor at a loss. Even more obvious, perhaps, is the strong competition for governmental funding, of which military firms have always managed to reap a large portion. Without a clearer understanding of the military firm's operation, national policy will be made under a cloak of ignorance.

In addition, such a theory is applicable to government procurement for other goods or services, where the customer is a bureaucratic department or

agency. As government activities broaden, an understanding of the mechanics of the procurement process
grows in importance.

Ira H. Kleinfeld

ACKNOWLEDGMENTS

For her invaluable assistance in transforming
a set of hypotheses into a working model, the author
owes great thanks to Mrs. K. Talmadge, Programmer
for the Rutgers Bureau of Economic Research. Also,
a note of gratitude is extended to Mrs. Yvonne
Sharper, who assisted in typing the final manuscript.

CONTENTS

Appendix   Page

xvi

LIST OF TABLES

LIST OF FIGURES

LIST OF ABBREVIATIONS

ASPR   Armed Services Procurement Regulation

DM   Decision-Maker

DN   Decision Number

DOD   Department of Defense

DSA   Defense Supply Agency

EDT&R   Experimental, Developmental, Test, and
           Research

GNP   Gross National Product

MIF   Military-Industrial Firm

NASA   National Aeronautics and Space Administration

NET   Negotiation Evaluation Technique

PDP   Project Definition Phase

PERT   Program Evaluation and Review Technique

PI   Index of Political Influence

RDTE   Research, Development, Test, and Evaluation

RFP   Request for Proposal

TA   Technological Advance Number

The Military-Industrial Firm

The business firm has been analyzed by economists for many years in an attempt to determine its
characteristics, relationships, environment, available strategies, constraints, and the like. This is,
of course, not at all surprising, since a firm is
the "key organization in business . . . which produces, exchanges and consumes."[1] A formal economic
theory of the firm has been developed that appears
to have the following principal features: The firm
has a goal (or goals) toward which it moves in a
"rational" manner; its function is to transform economic inputs into outputs in a given operating environment. The theory concentrates primarily on changes
in price and on quantity of the inputs and outputs.[2]

The goal, in the basic theory, is profit maximization. Rationality means that no decisions will
be made that detract from the achievement of this
goal. It also implies that all needed information
for this type of behavior is available to the decision-maker, including a complete understanding of
the environment in which the firm is functioning.
The transformation of inputs is analyzed quantita-
tively and qualitatively under marginal analysis to
determine both the volume of output and the "mix" of
inputs and outputs that maximizes profits. The result is that the entrepreneur-manager is expected to

behave in an "economizing" manner, making a transformation of "inputs to outputs of a higher order of
value."[3]

A number of alternate versions of this basic
theory have been proposed, based on dissatisfaction
with its assumptions and emphasis. One such alternative stems from the rejection of a single entrepreneurial goal--that of profit maximization. Thus, one
or more additional (dependent) variables will be added
to the model of business-firm behavior. Some of these
are: desire for leisure, maintaining control of the
firm, security of profits, maintenance of the firm's
share of the market, growth, and liquidity.[4] Another
alternative is motivated by the separation of ownership and management in modern corporations, wherein
the managers have an opportunity to set goals that may
be directly opposed to profit maximization. One such
approach views an acceptable level of profits as a
constraint on managerial goals of salary, security,
dominance, and professional excellence.[5]

Obviously, this is not an exhaustive classification of existing theories of the firm. However, all
existing economic theories of the firm feature "economizing," that is, the most efficient actions directed
toward achievement of these goals. Such theories do
not adequately apply to the type of firm that has
achieved a particular significance in our society--
the military-industrial firm (MIF) an enterprise that
sells highly technical products to the Department of
Defense (DOD).

DECISION-MAKING IN THE
CIVILIAN FIRM

There are a number of managerial decision-making
activities that, taken together, give the civilian
firm its individual characteristics and provide the
impetus for its success in the market place. Arthur
H. Cole identified six areas that, he claimed, "com-
prehend all the important phases of purpose in the
individual business unit, whether it be large or
small, or concerned with commercial, industrial,

banking or other business activities."   These are:

> the determination of the business objec-
> tives of the enterprise, and the change
> of those objectives as conditions require
> or make advantageous; the development and
> maintenance of an organization, including
> efficient relations with sub-ordinates and
> all employees; the securing of adequate
> financial resources, the retention of them,
> and the nurture of good relations with ex-
> isting and potential investors; the acqui-
> sition of efficient technological equipment,
> and the revision of it as new machinery
> appears; the development of a market for
> products, and the devision of new products
> to meet or anticipate consumer demands;
> and the maintenance of good relations with
> public authorities and with society at
> large.[6]

An important premise here is that there are meaningful choices available to the decision-maker.   While
the freedom of choice may not be unbounded in all of
the areas listed, there are usually many alternatives
available in each of them.   The economizing suggested
in the theory of the firm is the result of an optimal
selection from among these alternatives.   The sum of
the individual area choices should move the firm
closer to its goal (or goals) than any other possible
combination.

From within these rather broad channels of activity, the following more specific decision-making
requirements of an industrial firm have been selected
for this evaluation of the military-industrial firm:
What shall be produced?   What shall the specifications for the product/service be?   What quality attributes shall be selected for the various products/
services?   How shall these be tested?   What quantities
shall be produced?   How shall the product be distrib-
uted?   How shall the product be made?   What shall the
price be?   What will the working capital requirements
be and how shall they be met?   What investments shall
be made in plant, equipment, research, etc.?

This list certainly does not exhaust Cole's
list, but it contains enough of the critical managerial activities found in the civilian firm to support the following claim: If an enterprise does not
have freedom of choice in most of these areas, and/or
if the majority of these decisions are made for it by
outside agencies, then the classic free-enterprise
theories of the firm will not apply to it in a meaningful way and it should be considered a different
entity.

A DEFINITION OF THE MIF

This study will show that the military-industrial firm either does not have decision-making autonomy in the areas listed above or else that it is
not really necessary for it to be concerned about
them. In so doing, it will be demonstrated that the
MIF does not belong in the category of free-enterprise firms and that the need exists for a special
theory to describe its functioning.

For the purpose of this study, the MIF shall be
defined as any organization that acts as a supplier
for the military establishment and satisfies the following conditions: The problems and projects worked
on are complex and require considerable innovation
for their completion; the effort expended upon them
requires the coordinated effort of scientists and
engineers, whose contribution constitutes a significant part of the total venture; and the company
functions in a monopsonistic situation, i.e., there
is only one customer, the Department of Defense.

This definition is based on characteristics of
product and customer. Thus, the MIF would cease to
exist if all contracts with the DOD were terminated
and the company started mass producing a consumer
item. Also, it is possible to include with this
definition a division, plant, or some other portion
of a company that is engaged in both military and
civilian work, since only contributors to the DOD
product are members of the MIF. Activities such as
university research or research performed by non-profit

organizations may be included. Finally, it is clear
that a theory of the MIF may be applied to the increasing number of companies doing work for other
government agencies, notably the National Aeronautics
and Space Administration (NASA).

A large portion of MIF activity is financed by
DOD contracts classified as Experimental, Developmental, Test, and Research (EDT&R). The breakdown
of EDT&R expenditures by the DOD (based on the budget
programs for Fiscal Year 1970) is as follows: 4.4
percent Research (increased knowledge of natural
phenomena); 12.3 percent Exploratory Development (effort directed toward the solution of specific military problems short of major development projects);
12.9 percent Advanced Development (projects that have
moved into the development of hardware for experimental or engineering test); 14 percent Engineering
Development (programs being engineered for service
use but not yet approved for procurement or operation); 39.7 percent Operational Systems Development
(research and development effort directed toward
development, engineering, and test of systems that
have been approved for production and service employment, but otherwise have the same characteristics as
engineering-development programs); 16.7 percent Management and Support (effort in support of installations or operations required for general research
and development use, such as test ranges and maintenance support of laboratories).[7]

Consideration will not be given to suppliers
such as dairies selling ice cream and milk to military installations, clothing manufacturers making
uniforms, construction contractors building troop
barracks, or truck manufacturers supplying standard
or only slightly modified diesel engines. The reasons for excluding these companies are that their
DOD activities are often mere extensions of their
functioning in the civilian economy. While their
military business operates under a different set of
rules, these do not exert a significant influence on
their principal management activities. The mutation
of these firms is not as complete as it is for those
included by our definition--their activities are
totally bounded by DOD regulations.

THE MIF'S CUSTOMER

This discussion of the military includes its
three procurement agencies: Defense Supply Agency
(DSA), Defense Communications Agency, and Defense
Atomic Support Agency. Each of these is responsible
directly to the Secretary of Defense. In addition,
the study is concerned with the buying done by the
three operational branches: the Army, the Navy, and
the Air Force. At the next lower echelon, a military
official in each branch coordinates and directs the
over-all procurement operation.[8]

The basic law that governs defense procurement
is Title 10, Chapter 137 of the U.S. Code (herein-
after referred to as the "Procurement Act").[9] A
number of supplementary publications have been issued
by the DOD or its divisions to serve as instructions
and guides for this activity. Thus, we have the
Armed Services Procurement Regulation (ASPR), jointly
issued by the military departments, which is supposed
to provide uniform policies for carrying out provisions of the "Procurement Act" and to establish policies in areas not covered by it. There are also
departmental regulations that implement ASPR--the
Navy Procurement Directions, the Army Procurement
Procedures, and the Air Force Procurement Instructions. The DSA provides the Defense Supply Procurement Regulations. Finally, there are special
instructions, directives, circulars, notices, etc.,
issued both by the DOD and the military departments
to deal with special situations.

This brief description of the procurement organization and regulations is presented primarily to
give notice that a highly developed and systematized
buying function exists in the DOD and to suggest
that neither its power nor the extent of its influence should be considered accidental or fleeting.
This forms part of our demonstration that the critical decision-making areas of the civilian firm (as
listed in the previous section) do not apply to the
MIF.

THE MIF'S PRODUCT

The military customer will specify (usually in
great detail) the nature of the product he wishes to
buy. The DOD has prepared the Index of Specifications and Standards, which includes all military specifications and all governmental specifications used
by the Defense Department. If a firm wishes to become a supplier, it must produce according to these
specifications.

But, even where the nature of the work is not
readily amenable to standardization and specification,
the DOD attempts to approach the task in a way that
makes at least some circumscription possible. For
example, certain projects funded as Research, Development, Test, and Evaluation (RDTE) activities may
be required to engage in a Project Definition Phase
(PDP), which

> is a period of time set aside for precise
> planning of engineering, management, sched-
> ule, and cost factors. During PDP, the
> proposed project is analyzed in detail to
> derive more realistic estimates of what
> will be developed--how it will be devel-
> oped--how much it will cost--and how long
> it will take to complete.[10]

The influence of the DOD in determining the specifications for future (Phase II) work is clearly apparent.

The decisions on product quality are made by
the DOD customers, who have drawn up some detailed
procedures and standards. These describe the methods that will be used to control quality, and depend
on the complexity of the item. There is even a DOD
decision regarding where inspections are to take
place.

The importance of properly determining the quantities that the MIF shall produce and the assumption

of this responsibility by the DOD are understood in
the following instructions:

> Determination of the quantity of an item to
> be procured is the responsibility of the
> requesting activity. The activity makes
> this determination on the basis of approved
> program directives, regular supply-demand
> reviews, and other known requirements for
> the item. When the contracting officer re-
> ceives the request, he analyses the stated
> quantity for its contractual implications.
> He considers how quantities will affect
> price, competition, authority to negotiate,
> and so forth. He also determines whether
> the stated quantity makes it possible to
> implement certain Government policies--
> small business and labor surplus area par-
> ticipation in the procurement, for example;
> and maintaining or broadening the indus-
> trial base. In all these areas he coordi-
> nates, as necessary, with other specialists--
> technical, engineering, small business--
> before he proceeds with the procurement.[11]

The above paragraph also suggests the assumption by
the procurement official of responsibilities that
deal with regulating or influencing the general economy and that seems quite a departure from the mere
acquisition of military supplies. There is also evidence of a policy that seeks to expand the military-
industrial base by dividing the procurement among
several suppliers.

The DOD customer decides on the delivery point
of the order. The supplier is given specific instructions concerning this decision: "To determine whether
use of a Government bill of lading is more economi-
cal, solicitations should generally request prices
for both origin and destination delivery."[12]

Further concern with the methods of transportation manifests itself in the requirements that a review be made of current rates and planned volume of
government traffic to determine whether adjustments
in rates should be sought. Special rate adjustments
are provided for under the Interstate Commerce Act.

CONTROLS OVER THE MIF'S
PRODUCTION PROCESS

The control that is exercised by the DOD customer over the actual production process takes a variety of forms. We shall describe some of the more prominent ones.

In the award of contracts for research and development work, the DOD procurement office is told to ask for "technical proposals" in addition to price quotations. Those proposals should contain sufficient information to make possible an evaluation of

> a prospective contractor's understanding of the Government's requirement; his proposed method of approach in conducting the work; the major problem areas he expects to encounter and his plans for solving them; the types of scientific, technical, or engineering talent and the levels of effort that he proposes to devote to the work; the nature and scope of any consulting or subcontracting services he plans to employ; his past experience in similar technical areas or with comparable development projects; his other qualifications for performing the work.[13]

The evaluation, which really means approval or disapproval, obviously implies the authority to require changes if certain aspects of the proposal do not satisfy the DOD decision-maker (DM).

An obvious difficulty in maintaining control over progress and decision-making on highly technical projects is their complexity, which may require a multitude of simultaneous activities, often occurring at widely separated points. In an effort to minimize the inherent confusion of these projects, the DOD has required its contractors to institute formalized planning and control systems, the best known of which is probably the Program Evaluation and Review Technique (PERT). Specifically, PERT provides: (1) systematic, detailed planning and scheduling of

the program; (2) frequent, accurate progress reports;
(3) continuous, timely reports that identify potential problem areas where action can be taken at once
to avoid more serious problems later; and (4) a basis
for simulating alternatives and studying their impact
on the progress deadlines before implementation.[14]

A civilian firm very often must decide whether
a component shall be manufactured or purchased. But
the firm that acts as a supplier to the DOD must re-
alize that the customer has the power to make this
decision and will very often exercise this power.
Interestingly, the customer often uses this power as
a strategy for keeping the MIF in line while a price
is being negotiated.

The use of overtime and multishift work as a
form of increased resource allocation to projects or
products that require accelerated processing is a
clearly recognized option of the civilian firm's management. But the MIF must deal with a government
policy that holds overtime, extra-shift, and multishift work to a minimum. Requests for premium-pay
effort require sound justification and written government approval.

Although the DOD customer's control over quality
specifications has been described earlier, the extent
of this control may be great enough to influence the
process itself. Thus, on very complex projects, the
contractor may be required to conduct a reliability
program, such as the one specified by MIL-R-27542
(USAF), Reliability Program Requirement for Aerospace
Systems, Sub-systems, and Equipment. The latter
calls for reliability criteria concerning design,
program planning, program review, statistical methods, demonstration testing, manufacturing, failure
analysis, and so on. The contractor applies these
to his project and "then recommends a reliability
program that will suit the objectives of the procurement."[15]

While the restrictions imposed on the MIF in
determining the conditions of employment are not as
critical as some of the other aspects of the DOD-MIF

relationship, the fact remains that these restrictions do exist and add support for the argument that control over how a product is to be made belongs more to the DOD than to the MIF. The employment laws that apply specifically to performance on government contracts are: the Walsh-Healey Public Contracts Act (June 30, 1936), which sets standards for wage rates, hours of work, minimum age, health, and safety; the Contract Work Hours Standard Act (August 13, 1962), which requires overtime pay for laborers and mechanics working on certain government contracts; the Davis-Bacon Act (March 3, 1931), requiring payment of certain minimum wages for laborers and mechanics on construction contracts over $2,000 taking place in the United States; and the Copeland ("Anti-Kickback") Act (June 13, 1934), whose purpose is to prevent extortion of money from workers employed on construction work.[16] Not listed is the multitude of laws, regulations, and procedures that deal with security clearance and, thus, choice of employees.

The discussion has shown that the DOD has the right to approve or reject (and thus influence, if not determine) the production system to be used in manufacturing its products. Through its monitoring activity, the DOD is able, theoretically at least, to control the progress of production and has the authority to make significant decisions concerning future operations. Furthermore, certain important managerial decisions, such as make-or-buy and the design of reliability programs, may be made by the DOD customer. Finally, the MIF must follow DOD-set regulations in the matter of hours and working conditions.

SETTING THE PRODUCT PRICE

In the classic civilian firm, management has the responsibility to investigate the relationships between the prices of its products and the demand for them. It then is expected to exploit these relationships to the firm's advantage. But, in the MIF, there is an entirely different situation. Pricing is still a critical matter, but the approach to it

is not the same. This factor is the basis of one
aspect of our MIF theory and is given extended treatment in Chapter 2. It will simply be demonstrated
that the MIF does not have the same kind of autonomy
in this area that one usually finds in a civilian
firm.

In the first place, more than 80 percent of all
procurement by the DOD is done through negotiation.[17]
This automatically brings the DOD customer into price-
setting activities, which, in itself, might not be
too radical if the military negotiator had the same
goals as the firm. But, in reality, his objective
is quite different:

> The negotiator's pricing objective is to
> achieve a price that is fair and reasonable
> to both the contractor and the Government
> (ASPR 3-801.1 and 3-806). This may be de-
> fined as a price that provides the contrac-
> tor with an incentive to do a good job and
> does not impair his ability to perform.
> This does not mean, of course, that a fair
> and reasonable price is always determined
> solely by the contractor's costs to per-
> form. Other factors may affect the price.
> Nonmonetary advantages may accrue to the
> contractor. Or perhaps the contractor
> needs business during a slack period.
> Thus, a contract price may be reasonable
> even if less, at times, than the contrac-
> tor's normal "costs plus a fair profit."[18]

Now, consider the less than 20 percent of procurement done through the solicitation of bids and
the award of contracts on the basis of some fixed
price. If it could be assumed that the contract was
always awarded to the firm that submits the lowest
bid, then it could be seen that this is a situation
in which the MIF sets its own price in accordance
with conventional economic practices.

But, this is not the case. The award procedure
has the following qualification: To receive the
award, the lowest bidder must be "responsible."[19]

This responsibility is given further meaning in the
following instructions:

> Although procurement at the lowest cost may
> be highly advantageous (an) award solely on
> a price basis to a marginal low bidder is
> not justified. Prospective contractors
> must demonstrate their capability to per-
> form successfully. If the contracting of-
> ficer is unable to obtain enough information
> to permit an affirmative finding, he must
> make a determination that the contractor is
> not responsible. Doubt as to the contrac-
> tor's capabilities that cannot be resolved
> dictates a determination of nonresponsibil-
> ity.[20]

It is clear that the DOD is buying more than a
product. The same kind of extension of DOD managerial control over areas of internal MIF operation
demonstrated here was evident in previously described
activities. To facilitate this control, the military
customer requests that certain information be provided by the firm, such as detailed cost breakdowns
in support of contract offers and other pertinent
business or management data.

WORKING CAPITAL REQUIREMENTS AND
INVESTMENT DECISIONS

The civilian firm's cash flow is a priority concern of management. Inability to finance work-in-
process until it is converted into finished, delivered goods and payments are received has been a principal cause of business failures. Management must
anticipate its financing requirements and develop
effective sources of money supply under conditions
of substantial risk.

The DOD customer does not insist that its contractor face these uncertainties and problems.

To promote private financing, for example,
the Government permits the contractor to

assign his claim for payment. It may also
guarantee his private loans in suitable
cases. To reduce the need for such financing, the Government makes intermediate payments of two kinds: partial payments on
fixed-price contracts and interim payments
on cost-reimbursement procurements. These
increase the contractor's cash inflow from
the contract; thus, they reduce the amount
of working capital he must obtain from
other sources.

The Government may also provide direct
contract financing in appropriate instances.
Customary progress payments are used most
often. Unusual progress payments and advance payments are also available. All
three may be used in any combination that
is needed and justified by the financing
regulations, ASPR Appendix E. Contract
financing, too, may materially increase the
contractor's cash inflow. Thus, the Government and the contractor have considerable flexibility in ensuring adequate
working capital for the procurement.[21]

Management in the civilian firm must also decide
how to allocate its earnings toward the attainment
of multiple and conflicting goals. In military procurement, the customer often will provide the MIF
with the equivalent of capital investments in an effort to strengthen the supply base. (This subject
is discussed at length in Chapter 2 in connection
with another hypothesis of MIF operation.) The formal acceptance of this practice by the government
ties in with the apparent take-over of MIF management by the DOD.

As an example, the provision of government property for use in the performance of contracts is an
accepted DOD procedure. The provision of what is referred to as Government Furnished Property is done
to enable the contractor to meet the delivery or performance requirements. The government's failure to
deliver such property, once agreed to, may cause a

delay for which the contractor is excused. In such
cases, the contracting officer shall grant the contractor a reasonable extension of time in respect of
such delivery or performance dates.[22]

The military customer is aware of the power that
accrues to him as a result of this practice, and he
may be expected to use this to his advantage. The
mere threat of removal of Government Furnished Property that is idle or being used for commercial work
may soften the contractor's attitude toward current
negotiations.[23]

INADEQUACY OF PRESENT THEORY

The MIF has been shown to be highly dependent
on its customer (the DOD) for decisions relative to
product, process, and resources. In the civilian
firm, these decisions, for the most part, will be
made by the company's management, and their effectiveness will be shown in the market place. Of
course, some examples may be found (especially in
the case of industrial-goods producers) where inter-
actions between the supplier and the buyer are similar to DOD-MIF relations. Thus, there is no claim
of complete autonomy for the civilian firm. But any
situation in which the firm has abdicated as much of
its conventionally defined autonomy as has the MIF
must be recognized as one in which the classic theories of the firm would not be appropriate. The MIF,
then, cannot be expected to economize in the classic
sense.

This is not to say that the MIF does not try to
use its resources in the best possible way; the
choices open to it (whatever they may be) are not
the same as those available to the civilian firm.
The MIF obviously does care whether or not it makes
a profit, and it must be concerned with certain aspects of its performance that are determinants of
its success. The performance criteria it uses, however, are not identical with conventional analysis,
such as price-elasticity notions. The firm may find
that it is under less severe pressures to economize,

but it can not entirely overlook, for example, the
substitutability of its products by the DOD as a
major consideration in its operations. The point is
that its concern with such economization lies in
areas quite alien to those associated with the civilian firm.

A new sort of entity has come into being with
the MIF. It is not like the classic free-enterprise
firm, because it has lost much, if not most, of the
autonomy that is associated with the principal decision-making in the firm. Its relationship with the
government has an unusual duality. There is, first,
the role of the Department of Defense as customer
for the MIF's products. But the total dependence of
the MIF on the DOD for most of the decisions regarding product, process, distributions, etc. defines
yet another relationship. Figuratively, it may be
said that the Secretary of Defense functions as the
chief executive of the MIF, with the President of the
United States as chairman of the board. This delineation of the MIF will be developed in the chapters
that follow. At the moment, it is necessary only to
emphasize its almost complete dependence on the DOD
for decisions that are equivalent to basic policy
formulation in the free-enterprise system.

The singularity of the MIF has an additional
dimension--the relationship of the employee to management. A superficial examination of the MIF would
disclose no apparent discrepancy between the way it
applies the conventional management principles, such
as scalar authority, delegation, and unity of com-
mand, and their normal use in the civilian firm. But
the workers, as citizens and members of the electorate, vote for the "figurative" company president.
Through their senators and representatives they determine the amount of money that will be available
for the company's operation. These same elected
representatives may often be called upon to exert
some influence in attempts to favor a particular
plant, i.e., to see that it does not lose out in getting orders from the DOD. The successful continua-
tion of a political career may depend on such effort.

In addition, there is a strong similarity between
the relationship of the MIF and the DOD and that of
the producing enterprise and the central ministry in
a socialist economy such as, say, the Soviet Union.
Some further attention to this point will be given
in Appendix A. The principal reason for introducing
it now is to propose that a set of circumstances sur-
rounding the MIF's functioning have produced a mutation in the model of a free-enterprise firm.

CONSTRUCTING A THEORY OF THE MIF

The MIF needs a set of decision-making rules
that are unique and differ from those commonly associated with the civilian firm in a free-enterprise
system. It is the aim of this study to develop a
set of such rules after first identifying the principal decision-making situations. The result will
be a theory of the MIF, whose nature and value will
be discussed in the chapters that follow.

A theory of the MIF should satisfy certain requirements. It should be derived from observations
that lead to a set of hypotheses dealing with the
principal characteristics of the phenomenon it is intended to explain. The theory may be considered as
the totality of these hypotheses. It should possess
both internal and external logical consistency--
internally, from its assumptions; externally, from
other laws, theories, and facts. Finally, it should
be as simple as possible.[24]

From a study of the MIF's operations, it is possible to infer a set of five hypotheses dealing with
its principal decision-making activities.

Chapter 2 deals with what might be classified
as the MIF's marketing activities. In this area are
included two hypotheses. The MIF's basic product is
"competence" to invent and discover. The MIF's "selling" activity is really an attempt to influence the
customer's selection of a technical goal. Later in
the chapter, a hypothetical equivalent to civilian
pricing decisions emerges--the MIF's pricing activity

consists of mustering added resources from the government, giving the MIF a greater resource base than was available prior to negotiating contract prices. Chapter 2 ends with two more hypotheses, the first of which is the MIF version of capital investment and the second of which outlines the approach toward gaining competitive advantage. The first states that a prime MIF managerial effort is concerned with the acquisition of government-owned resources in support of a contract. The second holds that top management in the MIF attempts to profit from the political force inherent in the enterprise and attempts to increase its likelihood of winning contracts by effectively wielding this force.

The set of hypotheses that have been proposed for the MIF will be linked together, first conceptually and then in the form of an elementary model that will be simulated to observe its behavior under a variety of circumstances. In this way, the hypotheses will be integrated into a structure that can give some quantitative illustration of the MIF's functioning and allow identification of certain notions of stability.

Chapter 3 will set up a structural relationship among the MIF's decision-making activities, producing a dimensionless model of its functioning. It will outline the model used to define stability in the MIF and to test the effect on MIF's operation of some changes in its environment. Its conclusion will report on the experimentation with the simulation model. Chapter 4 will present the conclusions and suggest areas for further investigation. Finally, a brief comparison of the MIF with Soviet firms is presented in Appendix A.

The approach that shall be used is holistic in that the firm will be considered as either a single entity or a small group of specialized entities (e.g., engineering, sales, administration). Simple goals of maintaining a satisfactory volume of revenue from military contracts are postulated, and decision-making behavior is based upon a well-understood environment and is rational relative to it.

It is possible to associate this approach with
the three holistic concepts of the firm summarized
by McGuire--theories of the firm based on economic
principles, game theory, and cybernetics.[25] It is
concerned with the allocation of resources to activities in proportions that will produce the "best possible" yield, in the form of maximum revenue. The
action of competitors in the fight for contracts is
a force that is recognized and included in the model.
And, finally, the model will identify stability in
the MIF's success in attaining its goals, providing
feedback on activities that are not contributing adequately and making adjustments to bring them back
into line. In this sense, the approach is a "cyber-
netic" view of the firm.

While there will not be an in-depth study of
intergroup relationships nor of the conflict between
organizational and personal goals, there will be references to these and similar topics from behavioral
concepts of the firm.

REASONS FOR STUDYING THE MIF

There seems little doubt that military spending
will continue on a significant scale in the near future even if a long-overdue disarmament agreement can
be achieved. The lead time associated with disarmament is, unfortunately, quite long. A leveling-off
near the present figure seems to be the most commonly
held opinion among the forecasters.

Furthermore, although the EDT&R budget also
showed signs of becoming stable, the appropriation
for Fiscal Year 1969 was about 7.5 billion dollars.[26]
This represents a sizable amount of business and
shows that the DOD will continue to be a customer of
this special kind of output. The DOD decision-makers
who deal with these firms, their owners and managers,
and, most important, the public whose taxes finance
its transactions should all benefit from a better
understanding of its nature.

Any theory that can be developed for the MIF, if
the elements of its definition are strictly observed,

should also apply to any organization or part of an
organization whose customer might be some government
agency other than the DOD. For example, much of the
work done for NASA would seem to fit in very well.
And, since this agency is soon expected to reach and
maintain an annual budget of about $5 billion, the
value of a useful theory is clear.

But an even stronger motivation exists for studying the MIF. The National Science Foundation estimates that there will be a net increase of about
765,000 scientists and engineers in the next decade.
Job opportunities for these people or for those whom
they displace will not be found in defense industries,
which have ceased to grow. A limited number of contract awards will increase the likelihood that an
individual firm will be unable to replace all of its
completed contracts with new ones. This will mean a
reduction in work force leading to lay-offs of engineers and scientists. The effects of reduced opportunities in military work are underscored by the fact
that the federal government supports about 70 percent
of the nation's research and development effort. As
a matter of fact, there is great concern at the present time over recent lay-offs of scientists and engineers. The unemployment rate for engineers nearly
tripled between 1969 and 1970 (rising from 0.8 to
2.2 percent) despite the fact that some of these
workers took less attractive jobs in other fields.[27]

One should ask why these people are not immediately snapped up by civilian industry, especially in
those sectors of the economy that have been identified by Professor Seymour Melman as technologically
depleted: machine tool, sewing machines, shipbuild-
ing, and steel, among others.[28] It has been a rather
widely held view that the defense-industry engineer
suffers from a "trained incapacity" to perform commercial work, due to overspecialization and an over-
emphasis on performance and reliability characteristics.
While this has not been disproved, a survey conducted
prior to the most recent lay-off of engineers in the
Boston area concludes that "lower salaries and general lack of opportunities in the commercial field
appear to have been the major obstacles in transferring

from defense to commercial work."[29] These obstacles
reflect managerial decisions and a philosophy that
does not seem likely to change soon, no matter how
strong the competitive disadvantage becomes.

There is, however, reason to expect a change in
public policy regarding the many pressing and large-
scale civilian problems that we face as the result
of population expansion, increased industrialization,
and higher expectations with regard to our standard
of living. A beginning has been made by the state of
California, whose former Governor described some of
the ways that engineering manpower could apply itself
to the problems of the state. In the area of transportation, the systems engineers may study ways to
provide a complete transportation network within the
state, efficiently coupled with land, sea, and air
transportation from out of state; they may be asked
to design new ways to cope with the criminally and
mentally ill; and they may also have something to
contribute toward the design of a system to accurately
collect information on which government and industry
can base decisions for years ahead. Finally, these
engineers may be able to solve the problems associated with the state's inadequate and piecemeal development of a waste-disposal system.[30]

A similar awareness of this approach is exhib-
ited by the federal government, which has identified
the problem of mass transport on the northeastern
seaboard as one that deserved this kind of treatment.
The increased activity of the federal government in
activities of this sort must be considered likely
for at least two reasons: The state can not be expected to finance the size of the needed effort, and
most of the pressing social problems are not confined
within the boundaries of individual states.

Federal support of such projects would come
about more easily if disarmament were a reality.
But, even in the absence of such an event, stability
in the military budget, coupled with a more realistic allocation of our gross national product (GNP)
to social welfare, would enable us to exert a greater
social-welfare effort. The United States in 1969

spent 9 percent of its GNP for defense activities
(excluding veterans' benefits and services).[31] As
the United States moves into the trillion-dollar
economy, a proportional decline in military spending
would still make additional total sums available an-
nually.

The important point, however, is that if any
government agency, for example, Health, Education and
Welfare, were empowered to spend amounts of money
approximately equal in size to what the DOD is spending today, a counterpart of the MIF would probably
appear--unless its obvious defects were foreseen and
considered sufficient motivation for a change in the
system of government procurement. A principal purpose of this work is to call attention to the need
for such substantial change.

NOTES

1.   Joseph W. McGuire, _Theories of Business Be-
havior_ (Englewood Cliffs, N.J.: Prentice-Hall, Inc.,
1964), p. 47.

2.   _Ibid_.

3.   _Ibid_., p. 57.

4.   _Ibid_.

5.   Oliver E. Williamson, _The Economics of Dis-
cretionary Behavior: Managerial Objectives in a
Theory of the Firm_ (Englewood Cliffs, N.J.: Prentice-
Hall, Inc., 1964).

6.   Arthur H. Cole, "An Approach to the Study
of Entrepreneurship," in F. C. Lane and J. C.
Riemersma, eds., _Enterprise and Secular Change_ (Homewood, Ill.: Richard D. Irwin, Inc., 1953), pp. 185-
86.

7.   U.S. Congress, House, _Hearings_, before the
Subcommittee on Department of Defense of the Commit-
tee on Appropriations, 92d Cong., Part 6 (Washington,
D.C.: Government Printing Office, 1971), p. 38.

8. U.S. Department of Defense, _Defense Procurement Handbook_ (Washington, D.C.: Government
Printing Office, 1965).

9. U.S. Congress, "Procurement Act," 84th
Congress, 2nd Sess., 1956, Title 10 _U.S. Code_, Section 2301 _et. seq_.

10. U.S. Department of Defense, _Defense Procurement Handbook_, _op. cit_., p. II-3.

11. _Ibid_., p. II-29.

12. _Ibid_., p. IIF2b.

13. _Ibid_., p. II-45.

14. _Ibid_., p. XIIc6a.

15. _Ibid_., p. II-27.

16. _Ibid_., chap. 2, sec. L.

17. U.S. Congress, Joint Economic Committee,
Subcommittee on Federal Procurement and Regulation,
_Background Material on Economic Impact of Federal
Procurement--1966_ (Washington, D.C.: Government
Printing Office, 1966), p. 32.

18. U.S. Department of Defense, _Defense Procurement Handbook_, _op. cit_., p. IX-29.

19. _Ibid_., p. Idl.

20. _Ibid_., p. III-41.

21. _Ibid_., p. IV-39.

22. U.S. Department of Defense, _Armed Services
Procurement Regulations--1963 Edition_ (Washington,
D.C.: Government Printing Office, 1963).

23. U.S. Department of Defense, _Defense Procurement Handbook_, _op. cit_., p. IX-47.

24.   Based on material from C. West Churchman, _Prediction and Optimal Decision_ (Englewood Cliffs, N.J.:   Prentice-Hall, Inc., 1961); Richard M. Cyert and James G. March, _A Behavioral Theory of the Firm_ (Englewood Cliffs, N.J.:   Prentice-Hall, Inc., 1963); and McGuire, _op. cit_.

25.   McGuire, _op. cit_.

26.   U.S. Bureau of the Census, Statistical _Abstract of the U.S.:   1970_ (91st ed.; Washington, D.C., 1970), p. 246.

27.   U.S. Department of Labor, _Manpower Report of the President_ (Washington, D.C.:   Government Printing Office, April, 1971), p. 18.

28.   Seymour Melman, ed., "Military Emphasis Blamed for State of Economy," _A Strategy for American Security_ (New York, April, 1963).

29.   Joseph D. Mooney, "Displaced Engineers and Scientists: An Analysis of the Labor Market Adjustment of Professional Personnel" (unpublished Ph.D. dissertation, Massachusetts Institute of Technology, 1965), p. 143.

30.   Edmund G. Brown, address delivered at the UCLA Extension Symposium, Los Angeles, Calif., November 14, 1964.

31.   U.S. Bureau of the Census, _Statistical Abstract_, _op. cit_., p. 245.

2

MARKETING,
PRICING,
AND MANAGEMENT
IN THE MIF

The title of this chapter indicates the broad classification of decisions made in the civilian firm from which the MIF hypotheses shall be developed. These decisions include the question on what to produce, how much to produce, and how to market the goods. This chapter will also deal with a type of managerial decision that is often quite complex in the civilian firm--the price to be charged for the product. The determination of a price in the MIF is, in some ways, a simpler activity and the nature of the process is significantly different from the one in the civilian firm. Finally, this chapter will analyze the managerial acitvities relating to the function of acquiring resources and regulating their internal flows. These decisions are dependent upon the determination of how the product is to be produced and how much capital is required under the production plan.

MARKETING

Decision-Making and the MIF

Harold J. Sherman, in a study of marketing organizations in the defense/space industry, compared the basic marketing functions of that sector with

those performed in the civilian firm.[1] The functions
of "market delineation" and "product adjustment," as
these exist in the civilian firm, were examined for
counterpart activities in the MIF. Market delineation includes business economics and research, product research, and sales and market research. Product
adjustment refers to the determination of product
parameters or attributes. These two functions,
therefore, constitute the basis of the decision as
to what shall be produced. Combining the information
about the market place with an appraisal of customer
response to existing or newly developed products
gives the civilian firm some estimate of expected
sales. The market is normally an aggregate of individuals (or firms), each of whom (or which) may be
unique in all characteristics except that he (or it)
is a potential customer for the product. Through
some appropriate technique, it is possible to develop
information about the market in a probabilistic form,
with, of course, the chance of Type I or Type II
errors.*

Sherman identifies a significant difference in
the MIF, insofar as these two functions are concerned.
In the first place, he notes that product adjustment
is performed by the Request for Proposal (RFP), which
means that the customer himself sets the product
parameters. The market delineation in the MIF does
not include business economics and research, product
research, or sales and market research, but does
contain independent research and development and
systems analysis.

The marketing manager of one defense contracting
firm made the following comment:

We sell the skill and genius of our people,
the techniques and devices they conceive or
create, and the organized ability of our

_____

*A Type I error is that error made by the hypoth-
esis being tested and rejected in error. A Type II
error is that error made by failing to reject a hypothesis under test when it is, in fact, false.

companies to manage the production or
provision of these products and skills
as required by contract.[2]

It is easy to see that this description of the marketing effort in defense contracting stems logically from
our definition of the MIF. And, while there may seem
to be a strong underlying similarity in the military
and civilian market place based on the fact that both
contain the element of uncertainty, it is clear that
the uncertainty faced by the MIF is of a significantly
different nature. In the transaction between the MIF
and its customer, there is an absence of any conventional product. It is, of course, possible to see a
physical product eventually emerging from the MIF.
But this product does not motivate the purchase in
the same way that the perception of a product gener-
ates a sale for the civilian firm. At the time the
contract for MIF services is awarded, the final product is not well defined. The entire purpose of the
defense firm's effort is to develop something that
has not existed previously. The DOD customer and
the MIF are, in a very real way, dependent on what
"discovery and invention" may bring, with an obvious
relationship between advancement in this area and
the effectiveness of the resulting weapons system.
Thus, the thing that the customer is buying when he
deals with the MIF is the firm's ability to discover
and to invent. The purchaser is making a highly
subjective judgment in awarding a contract under
these circumstances; this is the "uncertainty" that
pervades these transactions. It is both unavoidable
and dominant in the relationship between the two.

This characteristic of the MIF's functioning
leads to a sharp difference between it and the civilian firm insofar as the goal of a continuing successful operation is concerned. Whereas the latter may
be hard pressed to regain the commercially favorable
attitude of customers, should it have performed
poorly, the MIF does not have this kind of problem.
In describing one attempt at the evaluation of contract awards, Frederick M. Scherer states that past
performance plays a relatively minor part in determining the MIF's liklihood of getting a new contract.

He identifies the more significant considerations:

> The "other factors" which normally re-
> ceive much greater weight in competition
> selection actions, including those with
> implicit rather than explicit criterion
> weighting, are the technical attractiveness
> of concepts and designs proposed by the
> competitors . . . and the extent to which
> prospective contractors have suitable tech-
> nical, managerial, and physical resources
> available. The exact balance of emphasis
> depends upon the type of selection action
> employed, reflecting such variables as the
> degree of technical uncertainty present
> and the government's program objectives.[3]

Thus, the MIF focuses its efforts toward those factors
that are weighed more heavily by the decision-maker
rather than toward building a reputation for good
performance.

It is not surprising that this combination of
the uncertainty associated with discovery and the
highly subjective nature of awarding contracts produces the emphasis described above. The decision-
maker who awards the contract has his own professional
reputation closely tied to his success in selecting
the "right" MIF. There are four reasons he acts the
way he does: First, each contract is a new venture,
with elements that have not appeared in any previous
one, or at least not in the same dimensions. Thus,
he is looking at a new situation each time, and the
fact that he tends to minimize the importance of what
has happened before can be understood. Second, the
great uncertainty associated with the contracts must
cause serious doubts about any competing firm's ability to do a better job. If the DM is certain that
the firm that received the award was technically most
competent to perform the work, then he would certainly
believe that, no matter how poor the performance, no
other firm could have done better. Third, there seems
to be greater pressure on the DM to justify an award
than to follow up on performances. Many politicians
are interested in learning why a firm in their dis-
trict did not get a contract, and technical competence

appears to be a more powerful argument (perhaps because it is less easily understood) than disqualifi-
cation because of poor performance. Finally, there
is a natural tendency for the DM to be wary of ad-
mitting past errors in the award of contracts, which
is, in effect, what he would be doing if he accused
a previous awardee of an inferior effort.

The MIF seeks to sell its potential of discovery
and invention, with each transaction representing a
successful sale of its image and, therefore, the
successful efforts of a group of image-makers. These
are the people who draw up the proposals and develop
prototypes that are meant to demonstrate the MIF's
ability to invent and discover. But they are usually
faced with competition from other MIF's who might have
slightly different ideas as to how these new product
ideas should be used. The competition for the MIF is
seen, therefore, as a series of parallel efforts to
convince the DM that their abilities plus their product ideas deserve available funding more than the
others.

As a result, the DM must select from among competing weapons systems while he is working under disadvantages. He is given no reliability guarantee on
the performance of the product nor even on the work
performances of the MIF. His own technical ability,
in the sense of evaluating competing proposals, must
be limited when compared singly with any of the specialized MIF teams with which he is dealing. Given
the budgetary limitations he normally faces, his
decision is going to be a very difficult one for him
unless he falls back on a relatively simple scheme
that is, at least superficially, defensible.

It can be seen that there has been an abdication
by the MIF of the basic decision of the choice of the
product, in favor of the governmental customer. Even
though the DM faces many difficulties in objectively
deciding to which firm to award a contract, he has
succeeded in channeling the MIF's efforts toward a
product goal that only he can authoritatively govern.
This is a radical departure from the operation of the
classic firm.

The decision as to how many units of a product shall be produced by the civilian firm will normally be based on a forecasting technique. Various limitations in technique combined with market instability make this a fine example of decision-making under risk. There is a possibility of errors in either the understatement or overstatement of actual demand. Under our definition of the MIF, such decisions are almost impossible. When the development of a weapons system has been completed to a point at which a stable design has emerged, then the production of additional units for inventory requires a minuscule scientific-engineering effort--precisely the type of effort that distinguishes the MIF from other manufacturing organizations.

The DOD has recognized this fact and has taken some action to "break out" production items, i.e., inviting firms other than the original prime contractor to bid on them. Scherer has identified three types of breakout:

> Type (1) breakout really involves no competition at all. The government simply buys directly from the original producer items which that producer has previously supplied indirectly under subcontract to a weapons system prime contractor. The motive for this kind of breakout is mainly to eliminate the prime contractor's profit as middleman. With type (2) breakout, the government not only eliminates the prime contractor as middleman, but also secures competition on the basis of price. The original subcontractor can retain its production role only if it submits the lowest responsive bid. Type (3) breakout occurs when the government breaks out not only specific component items, but a whole system for competitive bidding. Then even the prime contractor must defend its production role against potentially lower bidders.[4]

According to Scherer, the third type is rare, with only one instance being known.

The emergence of an item in a breakout does not
alter the fact that forecasting and deciding on the
number of units to be produced are absent from the
MIF's concern. Even if a weapons system becomes a
production item, the demand is rather firmly set by
budgetary considerations, and the only risk is the
unfulfilled expectation of additional orders or the
cancellation of a contract for some reason, such as
technological obsolescence. The MIF invests in
facilities, expecting to turn out a specific quantity
of weapons systems. If the number of units over
which this investment may be spread is less than anticipated, the MIF incurs a loss. The close relationship between the DOD and its contractors, however,
erases the apparent similarity between the MIF and
civilian firms with respect to errors in judgment and
unexpected occurrences. It is not unlikely for the
MIF to expect (and receive) some form of compensation
from the DOD for having taken what is considered, in
civilian firms, a very basic kind of entrepreneurial
risk.[5]

There is one interesting aspect of the MIF's
activity that might be proposed as a counterpart of
the decision on quantity. This is the matter of
product quality, i.e., performance characteristics,
physical features, and so on. The MIF faces risk if,
in submitting a proposal, it does not achieve high
enough quality (holding down the expected costs):
It may lose the contract to some competitor who has
not been as conservative. If quality is too high,
however, the MIF risks reaching a cost plateau that
is absurd, even to the government agency's DM.

In summation, the decision as to how many units
shall be purchased is made by the DM, with primary
regard for existing and anticipated budgetary restrictions. Even if the system is broken out for
production runs, these are also rather definitely
set by the DM. The only risk comparable to that
recognized in the forecasting activity of the civilian
firm is the possibility of a cut-back after a figure
has been set. But this situation, possible only when
a design has been stabilized, is rare.

The need for analyzing alternative channels of
distribution, although an important decision for the
civilian firm, is simply not posed to the MIF. Specifications for delivery of the final product are included in the terms of the contract that authorizes
the work to be performed. Even in situations where
the quantity and nature of the product are similiar
to those existing for civilian firms, the contractor
may have his system of distribution strictly determined for him under DOD regulations.[6]

First Hypothesis: Producing
Technical Competence

The preceding analysis of the MIF has emphasized
the lack of a product, in the conventional sense, as
the basis of the transaction between buyer and seller.
While a weapons system may eventually come into being,
the DM does not have a display of models from which
to choose. He is buying a firm's capacity, as he
evaluates it, to invent and discover. The evaluation
must be highly subjective, and it is of primary concern to the MIF that the DM's view of its ability be
as favorable as possible. The "selling" effort of
the MIF should, therefore, be described as an effort
to improve its "image" in the eyes of the DM. It is,
in fact, an attempt to increase the liklihood of
winning a contract in which the company is interested.
This, then, is the principal product of the MIF--
technical competence. It can be defined as the perception that the DM has of the MIF in terms of the
firm's ability to invent and discover. The successful development of competence is apparent through an
improvement in the MIF's relative competitive position measured by the probability of winning a contract.

The idea of technical competence is an important
element in our MIF model. This competence can be
achieved by either of the two principles involved:
The MIF might "generate" competence through real
technical advances, or, on a comparative basis, the
DM's perception of the MIF's competence may be changed
by any element that makes him view one firm as more
deserving of a contract award than another. The

MIF's approach toward the development of technical
competence can be illustrated by the fact that the
Lockheed Aircraft Corporation was estimated to have
spent about $75 million of its own money in the period
1964-66 to improve its competitive position in relation to the contract opportunities that it viewed as
likely to materialize. For example, more than 1,000
employees were working on the C-5A proposal.[7] Similarly, H. J. Black, Director of Engineering and Development at the Aerospace Structures Division of
the Avco Corporation, stated that the research that
was conducted in his division was intended to boost
its chances for obtaining new business.[8] C. F. Horne
observes that "18% of the defense industry's top
scientific and engineering talent is working on competitive proposals rather than actual execution of
programs."[9]

     This leads us into the second aspect of compe-
tence, the contribution made by the DM. His perception of the MIF's competence is, of course, the only
thing that matters, since he will normally award the
contract on this basis. The complex nature of the
proposals he deals with makes his evaluation of the
relative merits of competing firms quite a task and
is, of necessity, quite subjective. As Scherer puts
it, "the uncertainties associated with a technically
ambitious set of military requirements may be so
great that government decision makers cannot select
the best or near-best technical proposal with any
degree of confidence."[10] The effect of the subjec-
tivity that is inherent in the process of selecting
the firm that will win a contract may be considered
a probabilistic system in which technical advance by
the MIF will increase its chances of getting a contract but will by no means make it a certainty. If
it is possible to think in terms of an absolute scale
of technical advance, the MIF that has allocated resources in so successful a manner as to have out-
distanced its competitors in developing technical
ability should have a greater likelihood of winning a
contract, but the possibility remains that it will
not get it because of some bias on the part of the
DM.

The inferences drawn from the above references
and observations now make it possible to state the
following hypothesis: The continuing successful
operation of the MIF is dependent upon an uninter-
rupted flow of orders into the firm. One of its
principal decisions, therefore, must be the allocation of resources to the development of new technical
competence. It is necessary to convince the DM that
the MIF can do the job of inventing and discovering
in a way that will satisfy the DM's goals. This is
the decision that corresponds most nearly to the determination of what shall be produced by the civilian
firm.

Second Hypothesis: Selling a Technical Goal

There are two features of the MIF operation that
lead to unique relationships and requirements. First,
the market structure can be characterized as a monopsony. This facilitates interaction and communication
between producer and consumer. Second, the product
that the customer may buy is not well defined; in
fact, it can be described only in general terms or by
vague performance requirements. The DM must confront
many firms, each of which has developed a high degree
of advanced technological specialization as a result
of work it has done under contract and also through
research it has conducted on its own in an effort to
make just this kind of impression on the DM. It is
neither necessary nor fair to deprecate the abilities
of the DM in this situation. He is not a practicing
researcher, and, even if he were, he could not match
the efforts of a number of teams working with more
ample resources. The DM's involvement with the contract extends to the selection of a technical route
to be pursued; he must depend on an appraisal of the
MIF that includes many subjective considerations.

The interchange of information between the MIF
and the DM produces ideas for future purchases by
the DM. These ideas stem from a combination of requests by the military and/or evidence of enemy
weapons achievements; they also result from suggestions by one or more MIF's, based on their techno-

logical or research advances and/or available skills.
The idea that the DM is dependent, to some extent, on
suggestions from the MIF in formulating the technical
basis of future contracts is recognized by John J.
Kennedy in his study of the defense industry: "There
are two kinds of proposals: solicited and unsolic-
ited. Solicited proposals are those in response to
requests for bids issued by the government; unsolic-
ited proposals are suggested programs unilaterally
submitted at the initiative of the contractor."[11]

The MIF, in its selling efforts, must obviously
have some perception of its "sales possibilities" in
terms of the likelihood that it will obtain a future
contract. A classification of the conceivable situations is provided by the following:

> The Marketing Potential Report (MPR) is an
> organized listing of the valid business
> opportunities. Each business opportunity
> is established in a classification which
> has to do with the probability of that
> business opportunity turning into a con-
> tract for Co. X. The higher the classi-
> fication number, the farther from a con-
> tract. There are five business classifi-
> cations, and they are established as
> follows:
>
> Classification I. A business opportunity
> in this classification is one wherein the
> final technical and cost proposals have
> been made to the procuring agency. The
> procuring agency has approved award of
> the contract to be Co. X. The only things
> standing between Co. X and contract proper
> are negotiate of the contract and its sign-
> ing. This is a Class 1 opportunity and
> has all of the characteristics of other
> classifications and in addition to these
> listed above.
>
> Classification II. A Class II opportunity
> is essentially a sole-source opportunity
> for Co. X wherein the decision to place the

business with us has been made, but final
proposals have not been submitted and/or
approved by the customer prior to award.
Action remaining for this business classification are the preparation of final technical and cost proposals, the successful
negotiation of the contract, and its re-
ceipt. The key characteristic of Class
II business opportunity is its sole-source
nature. At this point, an opportunity
must be headed for us and no other potential contractor.

Classification III. In this classification, the following minimum information
must be established in order that the
classification be valid:

The opportunity must be a part of an
approved program.

The opportunity must be approved for
funding and the funding available to
the procuring agency for use on the
program.

We must have clearly identified the line
of technical approval of a proposal and a
line of contractual or procurement approval of the proposal including the names
of personnel involved and their position
in the organization from the responsibility
standpoint of the approval. Additionally,
a strong Class III opportunity is one
wherein we have done previous work in influencing the specification to our advantage, injecting proprietary Co. X processes,
ideas or products to orient the procurement
in our direction, engaged heavily in "loss-
point" activity concerning competitors, and
generally oriented the procurement in our
direction by previous activity. Action remaining on a Class III opportunity is the
preparation of detailed proposals, including cost proposals and subsequent work with

the customer to bring the opportunity
to the decision in our favor, where-
upon it becomes a Class II opportunity.
An RFP issued by a procuring agency and
received by us is one normally expected
to be found in Class III. However, in
order to qualify, it is of prime importance that we have done preliminary work
with the customer concerning working to
influence technical portions of the RFP
in our favor.

Classification IV. This classification
of opportunity is one wherein one or
more required characteristics of Class
III are missing. That is, the program
may be approved but not funded, the program may be funded but not well-defined,
a requirement may exist but may not be
stated, we may not know in complete enough
detail the customer organization in order
to influence the procurement properly into
a Class III. A majority of valid business
opportunities will begin their history of
marketing activity in Class IV. In this
class it is difficult to justify proposal
activity beyond the preliminary proposal
phase. This classification is pursued
more by marketing personnel than by engineering personnel and is characterized
by deep investigation on the part of the
Applications Engineer to determine the
information required and the conduct of
the necessary influence to make it a
valid Class III opportunity.

Classification V. This category of business describes a wide range of activity
on the part of customer, wherein programs
are in an evolutionary stage. Programs
may be ill-defined, budgets may be difficult to determine, procurement agencies
may be unaware of the desirousness of
technical personnel, etc. A great number
of business opportunities will make their

      appearance in this category and will be
followed by the marketing personnel by
the technique of sales calls, investiga-
tions, the use of brochures, data sheets,
existing technical information, similar
proposals made for other personnel, etc.
It is important to remember that, lacking
the information we require to determine
the validity of the opportunity, it will
be difficult to justify a large amount of
proposal effort until sufficient investigation and development of the opportunity
can raise it to a higher classification.
To be listed at all on the MPR as a Class
V opportunity, the potential business must
pass the test of having at least a 10%
chance of eventual Co. X award and be
sufficiently identified that the Applications Engineer can assign within a factor
of 2, an estimated selling price for the
program.[12]

This listing exhibits two aspects of the marketing
effort. The lower classifications represent contract
possibilities in which the firm has developed competence, while the higher classifications represent only
opportunities for contracts and, therefore, alternative strategies for allocation of resources to influence the DM in a direction more favorable to the
firm.

      The problem that faces the MIF in allocating its
resources to best advantage under these circumstances
have been described by Merton Peck and Frederick
Scherer. The MIF, they observe, will tend to stress
existing programs, both in qualitative (program-
management) and quantitative (technical) areas. To
create future program opportunities, however, there
is a tendency for qualitative talent in technical
fields to do advanced work in areas that have not
yet reached program status.[13] Diversion of technical
manpower from contracts that have been won to work
on proposals and other evidence of competence was
noted in connection with the first hypothesis. The
above observation is offered to strengthen the notion

that the MIF, functioning in an environment that
does not (or can not) give heavy weighting to actual
performance, emphasizes "promise", in the form of
product ideas and performance potential.

That the purchasing authority is vested in a
military agency, that the technical base of future
contracts is highly unsettled, and that the art of
persuasion is a key factor in shaping the DM's choice
of technical objectives lead to conclusions about
the composition of the MIF's selling team. Quite
often it will consist of a retired military officer,
whose principal purpose is, of course, making contact with the military administration; one or more
engineers or scientists competent in the relevant
areas of technology, whose communication with their
DM counterparts is made easier by this contact; and
a "sales type," whose purpose appears to be the cre-
ation of a congenial atmosphere in which the acquisition of information may take place. The composition of this team and its relationship with the DM
are ideal for its dual purpose of finding out what
the customer does want and pointing out what the
customer might want.

Regarding the first member of the team (the
retired military officer), a congressional hearing
made some interesting discoveries:

More than 1,400 retired officers in the
rank of major or higher--including 261
of general or flag rank--were found to
be employed by the top 100 defense contractors. The company employing the
largest number (187, including 27 retired generals and admirals) was General
Dynamics Corp., headed by former Secretary
of the Army, Frank Pace, which also received the biggest defense orders of any
company in 1960. Duties of these officers,
according to the testimony of their employers, encompassed a wide range of technical management, and "representation"
functions.

The need for technical people on the sales team does
not need any explanation. But the presence of a
sales type may seem surprising in view of the apparent
lack of product interchangeability and the presumed
motivation of the DM. Surprise vanishes when one
considers that the MIF has found from experience
that close personal contacts between its sales team
and the DM cannot hurt its chances for obtaining contracts; in fact, they may be necessary when competing
firms are active in seeking beneficial social relations.

The inferences that may be drawn from the earlier
portions of this section lead to the second hypothesis: The "selling effort" of the MIF consists of an
exchange of ideas and technical information between
it and the DM. Opportunities for future contracts
begin with ideas that are attractive to the DM and
progress through a sequence of stages in which the
MIF's likelihood of realizing an eventual contract
may increase or decrease. It is obviously in the
best interests of the firm to direct the customer's
thinking and preferences into areas where he will
perceive the MIF's competence as superior to that of
other firms. In order to accomplish this, resources
must be expended to fund a team consisting of personnel who have access to the DM, who are able to
communicate technical ideas very fluently, and who
have the knack of developing an atmosphere that is
conducive to the free flow of this information.

Summary

Two hypotheses were developed that deal with
what would be called marketing activities in the
civilian firm. The product of the MIF was defined
as technical competence, which often is translated
into technical proposals for work to which the DM
has decided to commit funds. The firm will often
allocate substantial resources to the development
of such proposals.

But there is more to the business of getting
contracts than the preparation of proposals. The
product area is highly technical, leading to

uncertainties on the part of the DM about which one of several rapidly evolving directions should be followed in acquiring new weapons systems. It is essential that the MIF try to steer the DM into technical areas it has been developing. And it is also important that the MIF have advance warning of any strong preferences the DM may already have. This selling effort apparently requires three components that are also present in the civilian situation: access, fluent and persuasive promulgation of product characteristics, and a congenial atmosphere. In the MIF, however, they may take on special forms.

PRICING

The Civilian Firm

In the situation that economists define as pure competition, the market sets the price. A condition of stability exists that is the net effect of such factors as a given technological knowledge or relatively small continuous changes in technology, the fixed nature of product attributes and the resulting lack of any real discrimination among products, the ease of entry into the industry and the large number of firms, and the lack of substitute products. But a situation like this rarely occurs, even as an approximation, and it certainly does not exist for the MIF. It is necessary, therefore, to explore some deviations from this condition that exist in civilian activities and that are more representative of the kind of pricing problems that are faced by the MIF. Joel Dean has identified those conditions that determine how much price discretion a seller has available to him.[14] The remainder of this discussion on pricing practices in the civilian firm will be based on his analysis.

Some of the factors that determine a firm's freedom to set its own prices are the number of competitors who sell functionally similar products, the likelihood that the market will attract new firms, and the degree of physical difference between the seller's product and those of other companies.

These three factors are significant elements in the
MIF's operation. Pricing will now be considered in
two situations where civilian firms have attributes
quite similar to those of the MIF--monopoly pricing
and pioneer pricing. A third situation--that of a
monopsony in the civilian market--will also be considered.

The MIF may be likened in some ways to the
monopoly in the civilian market. There are usually
no immediate substitutes for its military products,
which have won acceptance because of unique technical
attributes. The entry of other firms into competition at the time the contract is being awarded would
be impractical. Thus, it might be expected that the
MIF would set its prices much like the monopolistic
civilian firm.

The economic theory for monopoly pricing suggests
that there exists a relationship between price and
demand (in units) and a relationship between demand
(in units) and cost, as shown in Figure 1.[15] In this
example, the price that maximizes profit occurs at
300,000 units and represents the largest positive
remainder obtained when total costs are subtracted
from total revenues.

But the notion of pricing to maximize profit,
given cost and demand relationships, does not apply
to the MIF for several reasons. First, the quantity
that is to be produced is closely related to budgetary
considerations and, thus, not dependent on price in
the usual sense. Second, the cost function is almost
completely unknown at the time of sale. Finally, the
technical attractiveness of the proposal to the DM
would suggest price inelasticity, since performance
characteristics are more important than cost factors.
While the relationship between cost and revenue de-
picted in Figure 1 does not apply to the MIF, the
existence of some relationship cannot be denied
(this will be developed later in the chapter).
Although the exact costs at the completion of the
contract cannot be accurately predetermined, the
behavior of cost can be approximated by a curve,

stochastic in nature, with the abscissa representing
some notion of contract size. It is the revenue line
that forms the unique aspect of the MIF's functioning.

Another civilian firm whose activity might be
considered similar to the MIF's is the one that develops a radically new product "temporarily protected
from competition by patents, secrets of production,
control of a scarce resource, or by other barriers."[16]
Here, the firm's discretion in setting a price is due
to the differentiation between its product and others,
even though it might only be temporary. This "pioneer"

FIGURE 1

Relationships Between Sales, Costs, and Profits

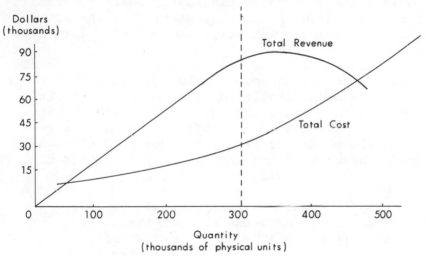

Source: Joel Dean, Managerial Economics (Englewood Cliffs, N.J.: Prentice-
Hall, Inc., 1951), p. 405.

has a choice between a "skimming price" and a "pene-
tration price."[17] The former exploits the commercial
advantages of the new product by going only after
that share of the market that would be willing to pay
high prices. The latter represents an attempt to
reach the mass market early and is based on the anticipated reaction of the total potential market to
the price.

But the MIF does not have this pair of alternatives, there being no mass market. And, even though
the MIF's dealings with the DM resemble a special
market, it cannot be characterized as a pioneer in
the same sense as in the civilian market. At the
point of sale, the DM does not have an alternative
in its procurement--weighing unit price and delivery
timetable. Rather, its choice involves its military
requirements and budget considerations. The result
of this decision is then transferred to the MIF as a
production order, with price and quantity determined.

A special form of cost-plus pricing in the civilian market is monopsony pricing. Since the MIF's
market has been identified as a monopsony, it is
important to compare the equivalent civilian situation. The example that is offered by Dean is the
automobile parts industry. But the tremendous difference between it and the military market is clearly
shown in the following description:

> [The automobile manufacturers] are in a
> position to make the product themselves
> if they don't like the seller's prices.
> But even here it is not the seller's own
> costs, but the costs that the buying
> automobile company would incur if it made
> the product itself that are relevant.
> Thus the seller's cost in this kind of
> pricing is only an indicator of the rele-
> vant basis for setting price that will
> keep competition out.[18]

The DM does not have his own production organization
that might take on the contract if a satisfactory
price is not reached. Furthermore, he has very little

idea of what the actual costs of the contract should
be. He is, therefore, unable to exercise the same
kind of restraint on his contract costs as the automobile manufacturer does on his parts costs.

Thus, the theory and practice of pricing in the
civilian market offers no counterpart to what goes
on in the military market. Even though it is possible
to identify some situations in the civilian market
that are superficially similar to the MIF's activities, there are enough basic differences in the two
environments to make the corresponding civilian pricing practices inapplicable.

Methods of Procurement
in the MIF

Title 10, Chapter 137 of the U.S. Code authorizes
two methods of procurement--formal advertising and
negotiation:

> The government issues an invitation to bid
> which must be sufficiently definite to per-
> mit all the bidders to submit bids on an
> equal basis. The invitation provides that
> the government has the right to accept it
> at any time within a given period, normally
> sixty days. Within the specified period of
> time the contractor is not allowed to with-
> draw his bid; this is the major departure
> of Formal Advertising in the government
> from normal contract law. Upon receipt of
> the bids the government maintains guard
> until the time specified for bid opening
> at which the award is made to the lowest
> responsive bidder.[19]

> The government specifies that negotiation
> is the process of verbal discussions to
> determine the terms and conditions under
> which the services or goods are to be pro-
> vided. It involves such elements as ob-
> jectives, positions, facts, issues,
> strength of bargaining parties, and strat-
> egy. The Services use the process of

negotiation in a variety of situations,
but the most frequent uses are in competitive and sole source negotiations
for aircraft, missiles, and electronic
systems.[20]

Title 10 states that formal advertising is the preferred method of procurement, but it also identifies
seventeen conditions under which negotiation may be
used (see Table 1). It is apparent that a number of
these conditions reflect the MIF's operating characteristics and would suggest that its dealings might
very often involve negotiation rather than advertising. Those most applicable to the MIF are conditions 10, 11, and 14.

The overwhelming dominance of negotiation as
the prime method for setting price can be illustrated
by the fact that in 1965 82 percent of the value of
military procurement was obtained through negotiation.[21] This is not an unusual figure. The conditions most heavily determining the reliance on
negotiation are impracticability of securing competition by formal advertising, EDT&R, or technical
or special supplies requiring unusual initial investment or extended period of preparation prior to
manufacture.

In his definition of negotiation, Kennedy mentioned the term "strategy." He elaborated on the
subject in another paper, presented some time after
the original definition was written:

The process of developing a strategy for
negotiation includes (1) the development
of specific procurement objectives, (2)
thorough preparation and accumulation and
analysis of data, (3) an adequate preparation for the physical organizational requirements, (4) selection of issues and
positions that will maximize achievement
of objectives, (5) the development of a
positive, constructive atmosphere, (6)
the development of aggressive leadership
of the session, (7) the development of

TABLE 1

Conditions Permitting Negotiation as a Method of
Procurement

---

1. National Emergency
   Labor surplus area and industry set-aside
   Small business set-aside (unilateral)
   Disaster area set-aside
   Experimental, development, or research less
      than $100,000
   Non-perishable subsistence
   Actions more than $1,000 but not more than
      $2,500
2. Public exigency
3. Purchases not more than $2,500
4. Personal or professional services
5. Services of educational institutions
6. Purchases outside the United States
7. Medicines or medical supplies
8. Supplies purchased for authorized resale
9. Perishable or non-perishable subsistence
10. Impracticable to secure competition by formal
      advertising
11. Experimental, developmental, or research
12. Classified purchases
13. Technical equipment requiring standardization
      and interchangeability of parts
14. Technical or specialized supplies requiring
      substantial initial investment or extended
      period of preparation for manufacture
15. Negotiation after advertising
16. Purchases to keep facilities available in the
      interest of national defense
17. Otherwise authorized by law

Source: U.S. Congress, "Procurement Act. 84th
Congress, 2nd Sess., 1964, Title 10, U.S. Code, Section 2304 et. seq.; John J. Kennedy, "Description
and Analysis of the Organization of the Firm in the
Defense Weapon Contract Industry" (unpublished Ph.D.
dissertation, Ohio State University, 1962), p. 33.

positive response through the introduction
of minor issues, (8) the acquisition of
information from the opposition to clarify
and test the accuracy of the identification
of issues and the reasonableness of positions, (9) the reclarification of issues
and positions based on data gathered in
prenegotiation session, and (10) selling
your positions.[22]

This concept of a negotiation strategy supports the
idea that the economic factors normally associated
with price determination in the civilian firm are
not appropriate here.

According to Kennedy, there are three factors
of importance in the MIF's negotiating effort. They
can be described as market intelligence, management,
and support.[23] The first of these can be simply
described as the attempt to find out how much money
the DM can actually spend on the contract in question.
Since the eventual "price" will depend on this amount,
it would be foolish to deny the importance of this
kind of intelligence work and even more foolish to
suggest it does not exist. The second factor, management, is, in the Kennedy view, composed of planning, organizing, and controlling the negotiation
session. The planning activity may be formalized
through the use of a Negotiation Evaluation Technique (NET) program, which is described as a PERT of
the projected negotiation decision process. Organization generally involves identification of team
members, the assignment of responsibilities, and the
provision of adequate physical facilities for the
actual negotiation. Control is the responsibility
of the team's directors and consists of adjustments
to the original plan as new information or positions
develop during the negotiation. The third factor,
support, is provided by experts in the various MIF
functions and activities. These are the people who
are qualified to defend the MIF's view of what the
price should be.

The staffing of the teams in one negotiating session was described by a MIF participant. Government

representatives were headed by the DM, a procurement
official with authority to award the contract (in
this case, an ex-Air Force officer). There were
government technical representatives (most of whom
had been involved in the preliminary activities described previously in this chapter). Finally, there
were members of the audit agency for the contractor's
area, who were present as experts on costs. The MIF
team was headed by a sales manager. Its support members were representatives from all aspects of the
organization: production, planning, engineering,
finance, cost estimating, and so on.

There are two comments that are relevant to this
aspect of the negotiation process. First, since support people have quite often been involved in the
preliminary work of developing the competence that
has won the contract for the MIF and have worked
continuously with the DM's technical people, they
should not expect too much opposition to their views.
Also, the extreme specialization of MIF support personnel gives them definite advantages in a discussion
of expected costs. Second, the DM, working generally
in a technical area that is broader than the one contract under consideration and hampered by budgetary
constraints for reviewing proposals, is not competent
to question very closely the assertions made by representatives of the MIF. The result of this situation is that management raises the target price set
within the organization by some amount and submits
it for negotiation with the DM. At the end of the
negotiation, the MIF is most likely to end up with
a lower price but one that closely approximates its
initial target.

The situation is further complicated by the in-
clusion of "change clauses" in the contracts. These
permit the DM to make unilateral changes in the performance requirements. But they also require that
adjustments be made in the contract price. According
to Admiral Hyman Rickover, "It is possible for a
shipbuilder to submit a low initial price in order
to get the contract, but finally end up with a prof-
itable contract as a result of changes and claims."[24]
Kennedy estimated the range in number of annual contract changes to be 500 to 17,000.[25]

Another difficulty--examining the MIF's cost-estimating data--was revealed by Admiral Rickover.

The Government encounters varied and constantly changing accounting systems. Extensive profits can be hidden in costs just by the way overhead is charged or how component parts or material are priced. The Government agency may never really know how much the equipment actually costs to produce and how much profit the contractor makes in producing it.

Most executive agencies have their own auditors who are supposed to take care of this problem, but they have neither the time nor the number of personnel to cope with the complexities and variables employed by industry which confuses the cost-profit picture.[26]

These observations on the negotiation process indicate that the DM is in a relatively weak bargaining position, which supports one of our earlier observations. One must not ignore, however, the close relationship between the DM and the MIF, which stems from and reinforces a common goal. The DM may not be sufficiently competent to question the cost figures supplied by the MIF, but even if he were competent, would he question them? To claim he would do so would be to ignore all the activity that transpired prior to the contract award.

If the MIF benefits from the DM's inability to track down actual costs, then it follows that the obfuscation of these costs is to the firm's advantage. Information flow, therefore, may be considered a technical activity in the MIF, in the sense that it contributes to the firm's strength in its negotiations. This point will be considered again later. For the moment, it is sufficient to say that the MIF will benefit from the services of accountants who understand the system in which they are functioning and can produce numbers that will support any cost claims that the firm is pressing on the DM. It is

clear, then, that record-keeping is a function deserving the same careful staffing considerations as
the scientific and engineering activities. This
notion is supported by Kennedy, who states:

> The contract function is not a major
> element in commercial organizations.
> In the American Management Association
> study of one hundred large companies not
> a single company identified the activity.
> Authorities in the field or organization
> do not include it in the list of the major
> functions of industrial concerns. The
> contract function for defense contractors
> is an outgrowth of the government system
> of procurement, and it is an excellent
> example of functional emergence based
> upon the requirements of the environment.
>
> The contracts division is a key function
> in defense contracting. The contract de-
> fines the terms and conditions and pro-
> vides the environment within which the
> desired product or service must be pro-
> vided. The function is usually central-
> ized and located near the top of the
> organization. It is composed of contract
> negotiation, contract review, contract
> pricing, and contract administration; and
> it is often headed by a vice-president or
> other major executive. When grouped with
> other functions, it is usually aligned
> with marketing or the controller function.[27]

Third Hypothesis: Pricing as
a Process of Negotiation

The pricing of the MIF's contract work does not
result from the same economic factors that prevail in
the civilian market. Instead, it should be considered
as an extension of the close relationship and inter-
dependence that bind the DM and the MIF. Most of the
prices are set by negotiation, which is conducted by
teams representing the two parties. The technical
members of both sides are anxious to avoid any

disturbance of the working relationship they have
mutually fostered. It remains for the MIF to justify
the cost targets they have set as their objectives.
To accomplish this, enough resources are allocated
to the negotiating function to produce a position
that is credible to the "objective" members of the
DM's team. The targets themselves are established
by intelligence work that estimates the funds available to cover the program. Additional resources are
expended to increase the moneys received for the contract through negotiation for costs of changes and
additions. The pricing activity represents an important income-generating function.

CAPITAL MANAGEMENT

The Civilian Firm

In deciding whether it shall invest in a project
or facilities, the civilian firm may be in one of two
positions: The investment is needed to satisfy imposed requirements (e.g., by government agency) or to
remain in business (e.g., replacement of washed-out
section of a railroad's main line), or there are dis-
tinct alternatives available for the investment of
capital. The concern of this work is with the second
situation.

What is needed for effective capital management
is some technique for measuring prospective gains
from alternative investment opportunities. The rate-
of-return method provides a sound yardstick for this
purpose. In using it, one estimates the annual earnings from the investment over the life of the project
or facility. Then, the discount rate can be found
that, when applied to each of the annual earnings
over the life of the project, produces a sum equal
to the original investment. The discount rate that
produces this result makes the present value of the
future earnings equal to the investment. In effect,
capital outlays buys a series of future annual payments that are equivalent in value to the capital
outlay at the calculated discount rate. This is the
rate of return. With it, one can compare alternative

investment opportunities in a meaningful way. Other
things equal, the alternative investment yielding
the highest rate of return is the most desirable.

The MIF

Investment opportunities for the MIF are dependent on acquisition of additional contracts. This
process has been described previously in this chapter. In effect, it consists of selecting project
ideas that have good prospects of becoming contracts
and developing the competence needed for serious
consideration by the DM.

Decisions relating to products, such as which
new ones shall be produced and what their general
quality characteristics shall be, are normally made
in the higher levels of the civilian firm. The decision to manufacture the Edsel was made by top
management, and its quality ranking was well understood by those people (it was, in fact, one of the
reasons for going ahead), none of whom would participate in the actual design or fabrication. These
basic decisions are funneled down through the organization and lose their administrative properties
while taking on the characteristics of technical details.

The analagous decisions on products in the MIF
are considerably more complex and require practition-
ers who are technically well versed. The rapid change
in weapons technology requires one to participate
actively in its evolution or become obsolete. (Consider, for example, the estimate by R. P. Loomba that
the half-life of a graduate engineer is approximately
ten years and his suggestion that the engineer should
pursue not just one but three different careers during
his lifetime.[28] The significant decisions about the
MIF's investments in new contract opportunities,
therefore, have the following characteristics. First,
they must be made by people who understand the alternatives and who concurrently have authority to commit
resources (not necessarily formally) to the alternative
they think is best. These people will normally appear
in the formal-organization chart at a level that may

be three or four steps below the top. Second, they
are tied in with the information-exchange process
described previously in this chapter, since the
commitment of resources to develop new ideas may be
based either on an identification by the DM of his
future needs or on the expectation that the DM will
accept the ideas developed by the MIF as the basis
for future contract awards.

This decision-making process does not have the
orderliness of the rate-of-return technique described
earlier, nor does it involve large initial outlays.
It is, instead, a piecemeal process that can be
stopped whenever the uncertainties associated with
an investment related to a particular contract possibility become too great.

In their splendid pioneering study of conversion
possibilities for the airframe industry, James J.
McDonagh and Steven M. Zimmerman emphasized the use
of government-owned facilities by that industry. The
authors make the following comment on this situation:

> Several reasons are given for the continuance
> of the practice. The industry points out
> that, under the policy of limiting profits,
> the necessary capital cannot be obtained to
> purchase equipment. Also, the need for ex-
> cess capacity for war mobilization could
> not economically be maintained by a commer-
> cial organization. The third significant
> factor is the fluctuation of the workload
> of the individual companies. The sharp
> cutoffs often experienced in the industry
> could bankrupt a firm with privately owned
> facilities.[29]

These reasons support the notion that the major burden
of risk-bearing has been transferred to the DM, an
observation Murray L. Weidenbaum has also made.[30] The
DM is very much interested in making defense work
attractive enough to keep the MIF interested and active; provision of government-owned facilities is
just one plum.

The net effect of the practice of making government property available to the MIF is an increase in profit, as a percent of invested capital, to an amount greater than it would have been otherwise. Recent data do not clearly demonstrate that defense firms perform at profit rates (as percent of invested capital) that are comparable to similarly sized civilian firms. The granting of government property, however, does help the MIF raise its profit as percent of capital invested. Table 2 shows the amount of government property in the hands of defense contractors.

TABLE 2

Government Property Held by Contractors,
June 30, 1967
(in billions of dollars)

Type	Amount
Industrial plant equipment (mostly metalworking equipment costing over $1,000)	2.6
Other plant equipment costing less than $1,000 (furniture, office machines, etc.)	2.0
Materials, electronic gear, cloth, duck, sub-assemblies, parts, hardware, etc.	4.7
Real property (buildings, plants, etc.)	2.4
Special tooling and test equipment	3.0
Total	14.7

Source: U.S. Congress, Joint Economic Committee, Economy in Government Procurement and Property Management (Washington, D.C.: Government Printing Office, 1968).

There is one more aspect of this topic that de-
serves mention. Normally, one thinks in terms of
plant and equipment when discussing facilities. But
one of the most important investments in a technically
oriented firm is research. And it is clear that the
MIF stands to gain just as much from having access to
the results of government-sponsored research as it
does to physical facilities. In this way, the MIF
is able to achieve advances normally requiring large
outlays without actually risking any of its own capital. The idea of developing competence has been
heavily stressed. It may be, therefore, that having
research results available to it is even more attractive to a firm that is hard pressed for business than
the eventual prospects of plant and equipment. The
procedure for obtaining such results exists and there
is an awareness of it by the MIFs.

To sum up the links in the system of DOD procurements: The DM has no objective and formal guides
in the award of contracts that lead to discovery and
invention; he must depend on his perception of the
MIF's competence and on his ability to work with the
firm; the evaluation of his own performance is closely
linked to some general evaluation of the MIF's performance; it is in his interest to facilitate the
MIF's performance in any way he can. Thus, the widespread practice of supplying government facilities is
easy to understand. The MIF expects the DM to recognize and appreciate its availability and dependency,
it being treated more like a subordinate department
than an impersonal supplier.

Fourth Hypothesis: Capital
Management

The relationship between the DM and the MIF and
the mutuality of their goal in the contracting process produces an important mutation in the managerial
activity of resource accumulation. The MIF is faced
with capital-allocation problems similar to those
found in the civilian firm. But there is also an
important opportunity to get resources from the DM
to support work on contracts. These may take the

form of plant, machinery, equipment, and even the
results of government-sponsored research performed
by other firms. Whatever the nature of the resources
granted by the DM, they represent additions to the
MIF's capital in the sense that they have been obtained gratis and that, in the absence of the DM's
aid, they can only be acquired through the investment of its own funds. Therefore, an important
strategy for the MIF is the effort to get government-
owned resources to support a contract. This becomes
a prime managerial activity and the allocation of the
MIF's own resources to this effort is a legitimate
alternative for the management group.

Method of Production

In the civilian firm, the problem of determining
the nature of the production system is a critical one.
While it obviously is centered on identifying and
physically arranging the necessary work stations,
there are other decisions that "spill over" from this
principal one. There are, for example, questions of
quality and its measurement, assembling and shipment
of finished goods, inventories of raw materials, degree of decentralization that will determine the organizational form of the production process, necessary
record-keeping, forms of managerial control, and other
associated problems.

Some of these questions can be removed from consideration by recalling the original definition of
the MIF. For example, choice between a production
line and a job-shop organization doesn't have the
same significance for the MIF. In fact, such choices
may not have to be explicitly made. The head of the
Operations Department at Avco's Aerospace Structures
Division emphasized this point when he noted that in
Avco's commercial product line a thousand units with
very few parts may be produced, as opposed to one
unit with a thousand parts, which is characteristic
of their aerospace line. [31]

Where there is some phase of the production process in which a choice has to be made, one finds the

DM's role to be a highly dominant one. As Weidenbaum
puts it:

> The distinguishing role of the govern-
> mental customer also extends to the in-
> ternal operations of defense companies,
> covering such aspects as financial re-
> porting systems, industrial engineering
> and planning (the compulsory use of PERT/
> COST systems for example), limitations on
> the use of overtime, purchases from abroad,
> restrictions on charitable contributions,
> patents and pay rates. [32]

The dependence on the DM for meaningful process decisions can also be seen in the following comment made
by George Tweed, Jr., Corporate Director of Engineering, The Cubic Corporation: "We have to accomplish
stringent tests to assure quality control. If we try
to run an industrial product through the same production line, the military inspector . . . suspects that
we're going to try to substitute some of our cheap
industrial products for the military need." [33]

The determination of the contractor's expected
performance with respect to time of delivery, quality
of product, and cost represents the closest thing to
a decision on the method of production for the MIF.
Improving one of those attributes can be made only
at the expense of either one or both of the others
and is known as a "tradeoff." It is made with the
concurrence (expressed or tacit) of the DM and will
probably be a deliberate attempt at fuller attainment
of individual or joint goals of the MIF and the DM.
The implementation of the tradeoff is obviously a
technical decision and will, therefore, be made by
people in the MIF who understand the variables involved. It has already been stated that these individuals are normally located three or four levels
below the organization's apex.

Fifth Hypothesis: The Political
Role of the MIF

Top management in the MIF is unable to make
final decisions about products. Authority for these
decisions resides in the DM, and the principal

goal-setting activity of management in the civilian
firm has thus been turned over to an outside agency.
The idea suggested in Chapter 2 that the real top
management of the MIF can be traced through the
firm's technical decision-makers, the DM, the Secretary of Defense, and then on up to the President of
the United States, should be recalled. A dual structure of hierarchical relationships, therefore, exists
for the MIF, as shown in Figure 2.

       The principal role of MIF top management could
be shown by enlarging Figure 2 to show some additional significant relationships, which have been
mentioned in Chapter 1. The DM functions at the
pleasure of the Secretary of Defense, who is appointed by the President. The President owes his
position to an electorate whose membership includes
the MIF's employees and others in its locale who depend on the earnings of MIF employees for their own
economic well-being. In addition, the funds that
are made available to the DM are approved by Congress,
which is elected by the people. Representatives and
senators who are asked for such approval include those
members of the House and Senate who have been elected
from the districts or states in which the MIF is located.

       This adds detail to the special, dual kind of
authority relationships that exist for the MIF (and
that parallel the relationships found in a system of

FIGURE 2

Governmental Authority and the MIF

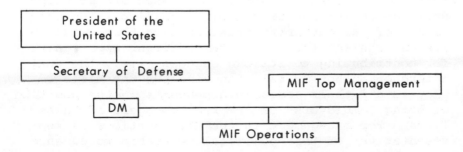

state socialism). But this set of relationships also
defines a network of personal political and career
goals of the individuals involved. It should, therefore, be recognized as a directory of people holding
positions of power, whose actions bear heavily on the
MIF's fortunes, and who, at the same time, are interested in maintaining the good will of those individuals who are directly or indirectly dependent
on the firm's economic well-being.

This provides a fertile field of activity for
the MIF's top management, who may seek certain political advantages for their firm in the competition
for defense contracts by approaching the executive
branch at a number of levels from DM on up, by
pressuring congressmen and senators and by appealing
to the general public locally or nationally. The
justification for their activity in trying to influence DOD decisions on contracts is always anchored
to an exposition of the merits of the program they
are trying to sell. But the unmistakable economic
and political implications of the decisions are never
far away. One technique that is used to influence
the political decision-maker, either directly, through
its message, or indirectly, through its impact on the
general electorate, is advertising. While this may
seem to be more appropriate for commercial products,
evidence exists that MIF management has confidence in
its value. MIF strategy is also directed toward en-
listing elected public officials in the fight to win
additional funds for particular programs.

Top management in the MIF is not able to function as the decision-making agency in areas of product selection or process design. It is, therefore,
forced to abdicate authority over what are principal
decision activities of the civilian firm. The unique
nature of the authority relationships that exist in
its environment leave it with different opportunities
for contributing to its own success--i.e., the dual
nature of authority relationships put the MIF's employees and their economic dependents in the position
of being "employers" of the real managers of these
firms. Top management in the MIF functions as representatives of this political ownership to advance

the firm's interests by increasing the likelihood of
winning new contracts. This activity may take several forms, but there is one underlying factor. Since
the work performed by the MIF is highly complex in
nature and the results cannot be adequately predicted
or evaluated, the claim of technical men can be in-
discriminately offered to support the more popular
objective of economic support for an area highly dependent on the firm. Thus, top management's efforts
may be described as the allocation of resources to
gain advantage over competitors when the technical
aspects of competing propositions are either equal
or indistinguishable. Putting it another way, the
political advantage that the MIF's management can
achieve represents an increase in the probability
that the firm will get a contract even though it can
demonstrate no clear technological superiority over
its competitors.

NOTES

1. Harold J. Sherman, "Marketing Organizations
in the Defense/Space Industry," in American Marketing
Association, Proceedings of the 48th National Conference (New York, 1965).

2. John M. Ault, "Establishing Meaningful Sales
Goals Under Uncertain Market Conditions," in American
Marketing Association, Proceedings of the 48th Na-
tional Conference (New York, 1965).

3. Frederick M. Scherer, The Weapons Acquisition
Process: Economic Incentives (Cambridge, Mass.:
Graduate School of Business Administration, Harvard
University, 1964), p. 69.

4. Ibid., p. 104.

5. Ibid., p. 115.

6. U.S. Congress, Joint Economic Committee,
Subcommittee on Federal Procurement and Regulation,
Background Material on Economic Impact of Federal
Procurement--1966 (Washington, D.C.: Government
Printing Office, March, 1966), pp. 50-51.

7.   John S. Gilmore and Dean C. Coddington, _Defense Industry Diversification_, U.S. Arms Control and Disarmament Agency Publication No. 30 (Washington, D.C.: Government Printing Office, January, 1966), pp. 86-87.

8.   _Ibid_., p. 280.

9.   Scherer, _op. cit_., p. 39.

10. _Ibid_., p. 41.

11. John J. Kennedy, "Description and Analysis of the Organization of the Firm in the Defense Weapon Contract Industry" (unpublished Ph.D. dissertation, Ohio State University, 1962), p. 86.

12. Gilmore and Coddington, _op. cit_., pp. 194-96.

13. Merton J. Peck and Frederick M. Scherer, _The Weapons Acquisition Process: An Economic Analysis_ (Cambridge, Mass.: Graduate School of Business Administration, Harvard University, 1962), pp. 506-7.

14. Joel Dean, _Managerial Economics_ (Englewood Cliffs, N.J.: Prentice-Hall, Inc., 1951).

15. _Ibid_., p. 405.

16. _Ibid_., p. 413.

17. _Ibid_., p. 419.

18. _Ibid_., p. 456.

19. Kennedy, _op. cit_., p. 30.

20. _Ibid_., p. 32.

21. U.S. Congress, Joint Economic Committee, Subcommittee on Federal Procurement and Regulation, _Impact of Federal Procurement--1966_, _op. cit_., p. 32.

22. John J. Kennedy, "Practice and Theory in Negotiation: A Conceptual Model for Negotiation,"

American Marketing Association, Proceedings of the
48th National Conference (New York, 1965), p. S-97.

23. Ibid., p. S-98.

24. U.S. Congress, House, Committee on Appropriations, Defense Appropriations for 1964, Hearings
before a Subcommittee of the Committee on Appropriations (Washington, D.C.: Government Printing Office,
1964), p. 8.

25. Kennedy, "The Firm in the Defense Weapon
Contract Industry," op. cit., p. 120.

26. U.S. Congress, House, Committee on Appropriations, Hearings, op. cit., p. 9.

27. Kennedy, "The Firm in the Defense Weapon
Contract Industry," op. cit., p. 110.

28. R. P. Loomba, Engineering Unemployment:
Whose Responsibility? (San Jose, Calif.: San Jose
State College, January 15, 1965).

29. James J. McDonagh and Steven M. Zimmerman,
"A Program for Civilian Diversification of the Air-
frame Industry," in U.S. Senate, Subcommittee on
Employment and Manpower of the Committee on Labor
and Public Welfare, Convertibility of Space and De-
fense Resources to Civilian Needs: A Search for New
Employment Potentials, Vol. II (Washington D.C.:
Government Printing Office, 1964, p. 1019.

30. Murray L. Weidenbaum, "The Defense/Space
Complex: Impact on Whom?" Challenge (April, 1965).

31. Gilmore and Coddington, op. cit., p. 52.

32. Weidenbaum, loc. cit.

33. Gilmore and Coddington, op. cit., p. 156.

3

A MODEL
OF
THE
MIF

This chapter will identify the principal components of the MIF model to be formulated. The model can be thought of as a logical construct used to study the interaction between the MIF and the DOD and the resultant changes that occur within the MIF. The model is, by definition, a simplification of reality, but it is designed to preserve the important characteristics. These follow from the hypotheses that were presented in the previous chapters. The task is to identify the components of the system that are of interest and to determine their interrelationships. Then, once the model has been formulated, it can be manipulated to observe its behavior under varying circumstances. If the model and its simulation have characterized the real system adequately, useful inferences can often be made. In this chapter, system components are discussed under two headings: internal allocation of resources and dealings with the external environment that produce changes in the operation of the MIF.

INTERNAL ALLOCATION OF RESOURCES

Webster defines resources as "available means; computable wealth in money, property, products, etc.; immediate and possible sources of revenue." The MIF's

resources consist of employed scientists, engineers,
technicians, production workers, accountants, retired
military officers, specialists in military sales, and
top management people who are influential in political
and military circles; research, production, and test
facilities; and money that is available to acquire
additional elements of the above. All of these certainly qualify as possible sources of income. No
distinction is made between various classes of resources, which is equivalent to assuming a quick
interchangeability (i.e., engineers can be laid off
to hire more retired military men or to buy new test
equipment). While this may be stretching things, it
does not contradict the basic nature of these resources, and it makes the anlaysis of the MIF much
simpler.

Technological Advance

The MIF must keep up with the rapid technological
advance that is an essential part of the market in
which it functions. It must progress rapidly in its
area of specialization so that the DM will give it
serious consideration when the time comes for awarding contracts. The probability of receiving a particular contract will depend very heavily upon the
state of technological development that the MIF has
achieved.

The Markov chain (Figure 3) provides a concise
mathematical structure for illustrating this process.
The states E_1, E_2, . . . E_n represent a sequence of
recognizable stages in the process of developing
technical capability, with E_2 being an advance over
E_1, E_3 an advance over E_2, etc. E_n is designated as
the most highly advanced stage the MIF would bother
to achieve without actually being granted the contract. The transition probabilities, which are the
elements of the matrix, each represent the probability
of advancing to the stage corresponding to the column
of its location in the matrix, from the stage corresponding to the row of its location in the matrix.
For example, P_{13} is the probability of advancing from
stage E_1 to stage E_3.

It is important to note that these states represent technological progress prior to the award of a contract. In this model, achievement of a given technological stage represents a deliberate attempt to develop a capability relevant to some future contract award. The process begins when the MIF learns through its information contacts with the DM that a contract in a given technological area has an excellent chance of being awarded. Some time after this, the responsible decision-maker in the MIF will begin allocating resources to developmental work in the appropriate area. This will consist of the assignment of scientists, engineers, and supporting technicians to do research and development work, build prototypes, test, and generate tangible evidence of the MIF's ability to satisfy the DM's requirements.

Ideally, the transition probabilities in this matrix depend on two factors. One will be the size of the resource allocation, since it is doubtlessly true that, within reasonable limits, the likelihood of success increases with effort expended. The

FIGURE 3

The Markov Chain

	E_1	E_2	E_3	. . .	E_{n-1}	E_n
E_1	P_{11}	P_{12}	P_{13}	. . .	$P_{1\ n-1}$	P_{1n}
E_2	0	P_{22}	P_{23}	. . .	$P_{2\ n-1}$	P_{2n}
E_3	0	0	P_{33}	. . .	$P_{3\ n-1}$	P_{3n}
.						
.						
.						
E_{n-1}	0	0	0	. . .	$P_{n-1\ n-1}$	$P_{n-1\ n}$
E_n	0	0	0	. . .	0	1

second will be the technical complexity of the proposed work, and here the relationship will be an
inverse one. That is, an increase in difficulty will
reduce the incremental contribution of an additional
resource unit. The matrix itself is shown to be tri-
angular. This means that all the transition probabilities below the main diagonal are zero--e.g.,
$P_{32}=0$, $P_{42}=0$, etc. This results from the fact that
the probability of regressing to a less-advanced
state is very small, if not actually zero.

The model will be evaluated over a number of time
intervals. At the end of each interval, a test is
made to determine if technical advance in state has
been made by the end of that interval. Two courses
of action are available to the MIF if there is a nega-
tive result. These are executed by a set of decision
rules. First, additional resources may be assigned
to the project. These may come from a "slack" that
is available elsewhere, suggesting that the MIF thinks
in terms of its inventory of resources, or they may
be transferred from some other activity (see below)
to which they had previously been assigned. Second,
the project might be dropped. The MIF, upon seeing
that its position is rather hopeless, might decide
to transfer its attention to another contract possibility that has come into being.

The contract award will be made by the DM on the
basis of a probability rule that depends on the state
of technological advance reached by the MIF plus other
considerations. Thus, there is a greater probability
of obtaining the contract if a more-advanced technical
stage is reached by the MIF. There is no deterministic, certain way that the MIF can guarantee winning,
however, for the purpose of the model, contract possibilities are treated as arriving at random intervals of time. They would normally vary as to technical complexity and size, but, for the purpose of
the model, all contracts are viewed as identical with
respect to complexity and size.

Production

Success in obtaining a contract commits the firm
to creating a tangible product, which may take the

form of a complete installation, research report,
test data, and so on. This means that a portion of
the MIF's resources must be allocated to this production activity. A dichotomous attitude on the part of
the firm toward this production requirement has been
identified, however. After the award, when allocating its available resources, the company might feel
secure in slighting production and concentrating on
the technological advance that increases the chances
of getting future contracts. On the other hand, the
MIF must recognize that there will be pressures for
some "reasonable" performance. There is a limit to
the extensions on delivery date that the MIF can expect to get. If there is a failure to meet specified
performance commitments, there are two possible results. If the delay is significant but does not exceed the promised delivery time by an excessive
amount, the MIF's "competence" will be reduced in
its attempts to get future orders. This will take
the form of a reduced probability of getting future
contracts, either for some fixed time interval or
until the firm is able to restore its image by satisfactory performance on a subsequent contract. If the
delay is excessive, it might lead to a cancellation
of the contract plus a reduction in "competence."

Thus, the MIF can be expected to view the allocation of resources for production as a rather flexible proposition. If it is hard pressed in getting
new contracts, a decision to switch resources from
production to technological development is a very
attractive alternative. This decision could be continued until the firm perceived that future contracts
might be jeopardized by poor performance caused by
the diversion of resources from production.

Each contract is defined in terms of a total
number of resources needed for completion and the
time intervals required. A certain portion of the
needed resources will have been expended in the
technological advance process price to the award of
the contract. The MIF that has advanced, say, to
the n-1 state of technological competence will have to
assign fewer resources to production after it gets
the contract than the firm that has advanced only to

the n-1 state. Practically speaking, this means that
a MIF in a lower state will have some catching up to
do as far as the technical requirements of the contract are concerned. And the production-resource
requirements per interval for this firm will be higher
than they would have been if the firm had achieved a
more-advanced state before it was awarded the contract. It is either that or a failure to meet promised delivery dates.

Production has some uncertainties connected with
it, just as technological advance did. Delays in the
output schedule, caused by difficulties that are un-
predictable and that will require speed-ups if they
become too frequent, may occur. Or, we may expect
unusual bursts of progress, which may put the firm
ahead of its schedule and give it some slack in resources available.

Summing up, the production phase of the MIF's
contract must have resources assigned to it. The
amount will depend on contract size relevant to delivery date and also on the state of advance the firm
reached before it was awarded the contract. Super-
imposed upon these two factors will be the possibility
of variation due to unknown chance causes, typical of
all production systems.

EXTERNAL ENVIRONMENT AND
RESOURCE ALLOCATION

Technological Exploration

The DM has a problem in determining what new
technical areas to investigate. For this reason,
the interchange of information between the DM and
the MIF is considered highly desirable by both parties. The resources of the MIF are producing, either
directly or as side effects, new possibilities for
technical exploration. Given that some general area
has been accepted by the DM as worthy of consideration for a contract, a number of alternative routes
toward the eventual goal exist in variety of method-
ologies, basic theoretical systems, and conceptions

of the end product. The negotiation of the contract
has been described as the culmination of the inter-
actions between the DM and the MIF in which the merits
of one of the alternatives described above have been
strongly defended by the technical members of the
MIF's team. If we recall the notion of technological
advances, the MIF's efforts at selling its own particular approach to a problem can be expressed very
simply. It is the process of moving the contract
specifications closer to the actual technical competence of the MIF. In the model, this will produce
some combination of the following: The MIF will
automatically be advanced one or more stages, and
the relative technical complexity of the project
will be decreased and, thus, fewer resource units
will be needed to achieve a technological advance.

The MIF attempts to influence the DM by allocating resources in the form of support for a properly
constituted selling team. In addition to the individual efforts of these teams, the MIF must be concerned with coordinating the total selling activity,
concentrating effort on those projects that seem to
offer the greatest prospects of success.

Political Activity

Situations in which political influence is ex-
erted in behalf of the MIF differ from the efforts
described above. In this case, the MIF is not concerned with changing the product or project content.
The purpose is simply to gain favor for the firm over
others that are either equal or superior in technical
competence. The immediate effect of successful effort is a change in the relationship between the
firm's technical competence and the probability of
winning the contract. The MIF's chances of getting
the contract, no matter what its technical state,
are increased. As a matter of fact, the probability
may approach certainty, regardless of the MIF's state,
if the political influence produces particularly beneficial results.

The net result for the MIF is not all positive,
however. By beginning "production" work at a lower

level of technical competence, it must be assumed
that the difficulties in carrying out contract provisions will be significantly increased. This
assumption results from the expectation that the
contract specifications will not be changed in def-
erence to the lesser abilities of the contractor.
Tying this in with the comments made on production,
we can see that the MIF will have to allocate more
resources to the carrying out of the contract requirements in order to escape the penalties stemming
from unsatisfactory performance. Political influence,
if it is successful, may bring a contract, but it
might prove harmful to the MIF's future prospects if
it causes a very poor production performance.

Negotiation for Additional Resources

Associated with each contract is a possibility
of increasing the return from a contract beyond what
was originally proposed. This may result from some
combination of the following: inflation of expected
costs and justification of additional charges, engineering changes, or some other deviation from
original program or estimates; acquisition of government-owned facilities, such as plant, equipment,
facilities, and services, as part of the contractual
agreement; and access to results of research and development done by other companies at government expense. The last has its principal impact when a firm
is trying to get into a new program area.

It is not difficult to anticipate the effects of
these three activities on the MIF operation. Each
case is equivalent to saving resources that would
otherwise have been expended. The MIF is thus able
to divert these savings into resource allocations
(described previously), including, of course, the
effort to gain additional resources.

Changes in Military Budgets

The MIF reacts to individual contract possibilities, and success or failure has been defined in terms
of individual contracts. But the rate at which these
contract opportunities occur will certainly have a

definite effect on the firm's operation. An abundance
of contracts would produce a backlog and a certain
stability in which some kind of balance is achieved
between various allocations. On the other hand, a
scarcity of contracts might produce a different set
of rules for resource allocation.

Summary

The success of the MIF is significantly influenced by its relations with the environment in which
it functions. The characteristics of this environment
are shaped by the monopsonistic market, uncertainty
of product and performance, considerable tactical
advantages of the seller in his dealings with the
buyer, the buyer's being subjected to continuous
political pressures and often forced to respond to
them, market volume for products of the MIF being
based upon economically irrational considerations,
success of a particular MIF performance being the
equivalent of a wise choice of contractor by the DM
(for which the converse is also true and much more
relevant--the DM is highly motivated to do what he
can to increase at least the appearance of successful
performance by the MIF), and the DM's interest in
having a "pool" of capable MIF's available to work
on contracts (concerning which, the DM is inclined to
yield to the requirements of prospective MIF's in
the development of this capability). In order to
function successfully in this environment, the firm
will have to allocate resources to the "marketing,"
"technical-information exchange," "political," and
"negotiation" functions.

In a similar way, other strategies may be expressed in terms of the resources allocated by the
MIF. The relationship between the amount of the
allocation and the probability of success cannot
be stated with any degree of certainty. But it is
not difficult to accept the following two propositions. A certain minimal amount of these allocations
must be expected at all times and will be a part of
a "steady state" condition of the firm. Under some
circumstances, the MIF might decide that particular
emphasis on one of these strategies is desirable.

FIGURE 4
MIF Model I

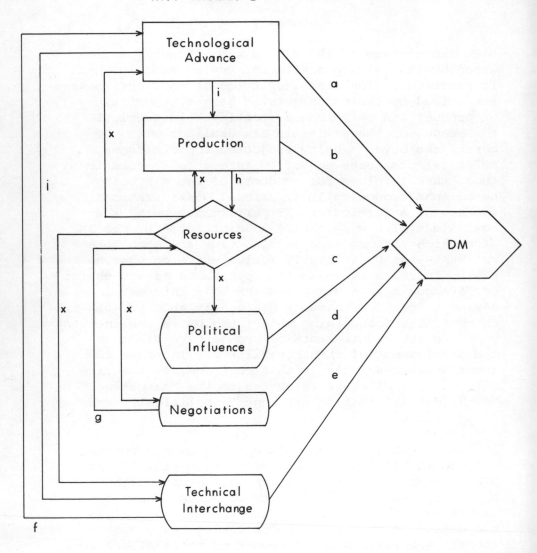

xAllocation of resources to the various activities.

aState of technological advance achieved by the MIF, which will determine the firm's probability of winning a contract.

bPerformance record of the MIF on "production" associated with contracts it has received. Satisfactory performance will maintain the firm's image of competence, but an unfavorable deviation from plan will negatively affect its chances of getting contracts.

cExerting pressure on the DM to award contracts on some basis other than ability increases the MIF's chances of winning a contract at a given state of technological advance.

dPressure on the DM, given that a contract has been or is about to be awarded, to increase resource flow to the MIF through increase in contract price or the buyer's contribution of resources toward the achievement of the contract objective.

eAttempts to change the original contract specifications to conform to certain achievements of the MIF.

fSuccess in having the contract specifications more nearly coincide with the MIF's unique abilities or accomplishments will make it easier for the firm to move to higher states of technological advance.

gIf negotiations are successful, the net effect is an increase in total resources available for allocation to individual activities.

hAllocation of resources to production may be considered flexible in that they may be withdrawn for reallocation if sufficient pressure exists.

iThe state of technological advance at the time the contract is awarded will determine the requirements of production.

jThe direction of technical influence will depend on the previous technical advance that the MIF has achieved.

It will then increase the allocation to that strategy
and expect a change in the outcome of its activities.

A MODEL OF THE MIF

From the preceding sections of this chapter, it
is possible to write the following equation express-
ing the central relationship in the MIF model:

$$R = r_t + r_p + r_i + r_m + r_n + r_s$$

where

R = total resources of the MIF
r_t = resources allocated to technological
advance
r_p = resources allocated to production on
contracts in hand
r_i = resources allocated to influencing DM
to accept MIF technical approach
r_m = resources allocated to political influence
r_n = resources allocated to negotiation
aimed at producing increased resources
r_s = slack resources, i.e., those not in
use at a particular time

Figure 4 shows the model's relationships sche-
matically, both in terms of the alternative resource-
allocation possibilities and the effects that these
are capable of producing. Some of these relationships
will be combined into a computer program that will be
used for an elementary simulation of the MIF's activities. Chapter 4 will give some of the details
of this program, while Chapter 5 will describe the
results of the simple manipulations of the programmed
model.

4

SIMULATION

OF

THE MODEL

OF

THE MIF

In this chapter, the computer program that was developed to simulate the MIF operation will be described. The purpose of this simulation is to provide an interpretation of the MIF's behavior with particular reference to the theory of the MIF as expressed in the five hypotheses. It also suggests avenues for further model building.

The simulation will proceed from an examination of the activities and attributes of the MIF over a long number of time intervals. At each interval of time, the status of the system will be measured and recorded, e.g., the number of contracts in the MIF's backlog, the contracts it is attempting to win, its technical advance on each contract, and the like. At the end of the simulation period, this running account will serve to indicate how the MIF has behaved.

The fact that the MIF is simulated over a long number of time intervals permits a probabilistic approach in the model. That is, certain events (such as winning contracts) can be treated as being influenced by the actions of the firm but still partly determined by chance. Over a long period of time, the random influences will serve to add reality to the model in that the relationship between DM and MIF is never entirely deterministic.

MIF CHARACTERISTICS INCLUDED
IN THE SIMULATION

Modification of Contract
Specifications

The marketing effort of the MIF involves col-
lecting information about the DM's attitudes and in-
clinations and attempting to influence him in a
direction favorable to the firm. If the DM acquires
an interest in an area of "discovery and innovation"
that has been partially explored by the MIF, then
his perception of the firm's competence will obviously be more favorable and the chances for obtaining
a contract are improved. The MIF thus has great in-
centive to convince the DM that its research has potential for product application. Simulating this
activity, which will be called modification of specifications, can be done by defining a probabilistic
function, relating the success that is realized in
influencing the DM and the resources allocated by
the MIF in the process. The MIF's effort is taken
to be successful if, in the view of the DM, there is
an advance in the MIF's competence to perform the
modified task. For the model, a number is defined
called the technological advance number (TA), which
will be an integer equal to, or greater than, zero.
An increase in this number will represent an increase
in the DM's perception of the MIF's competence to
perform on the contract in question.

In this model, the relationship between resources
expended and success in influencing the DM was chosen to have the following logical characteristics:
The total absence of resource allocation will result
in a zero probability of advancing the TA number,
ceteris paribus; the relationship is an increasing
function with a decreasing rate of increase. In
other words, each incremental addition of resources
to this effort will produce a greater probability of
technical advance, but successive equivalent additions result in proportionately smaller increases in
probability of advance. This is an embodiment of
the diminishing-returns principle; no amount of

resources allocated can ever produce a certain advance, i.e., a probability of advance equal to one. Thus, the function relating the two variables will have an asymptote less than, or equal to, one.

For the model, the function is

$$DN(1) = \frac{R_1}{A_1 + (B_1)\ (R_1)}$$

where decision number (DN) is solely a function of the resources used to effect a modification of specifications. R_1 is the quantity of resources allocated to this activity, while A_1 and B_1 are constants, greater than zero. A random number is chosen (from a hat, so to speak) and is compared to the decision number--DN(1). If the random number is less than or equal to the DN, we have a success. With success, the TA is increased by 1. It can readily be seen that when random numbers are drawn from a given source, increases in resources brought to bear by the MIF increase its probability of advancing the DM's perception of its competence.

The MIF is, of course, sensitive to the performance of its sales teams in modifying specifications. A contract possibility, as long as it remains under consideration, represents a potential source of revenue. If the TA is not advanced in a given time interval, there is an obvious motivation to increase the effort being applied to this activity. In the model, a simple decision rule is used: The failure to achieve an increase in the TA during any time interval will result in an increased resource allocation that is proportional to the number of elapsed time intervals from the emergence of the contract possibility.

Discontinuing Effort
on a Contract

A contract possibility must survive a test that compares its TA with that of other existing contract possibilities. If at any point in time an alternative

contract attains a higher TA, the MIF might stop giving its attention and resources to the less-promising
one.   During simulation, a record will be kept of
those contract possibilities that have been abandoned
and of the resources that had been allocated to them.
Another reason for abandoning a contract possibility
would be the size of the MIF's backlog.   After a certain number of time intervals, when the decision must
be made regarding development of further competence
in the contract's technical area, a satisfactory
backlog may result in a decision to give up further
efforts to obtain the contract.

Seeking Increased Competence

When the MIF has identified a promising contract
possibility and when its backlog is low enough to en-
courage the firm to compete vigorously, a decision
to seek increased competence in that area will result,
and resources will be allocated in the form of engineers and scientists to prepare proposals and prototypes.

A mathematical function of the same form that
was used to define the relationship between resources
and success in effecting modification of specifications will be used to determine the probability of
success in achieving further technical competence
within the MIF.   Thus,

$$DM(2) = \frac{R_2}{A_2 + (B_2)\ (R_2)}$$

where R_2 refers to resources allocated in this case
and A_2 and B_2 are constants.   They will be of a different order of magnitude from A_1 and B_1, however,
because this effort will normally involve a greater
allocation of resources than in the previous case.
The test of success will be of the same form as that
described previously.   That is, DN(2), which is
solely determined by the resources expended, is compared to a number chosen at random from a finite
pool.   If the random number is less than, or equal
to, the DN(2), an increment in the TA results.   This

denotes an advance in the DM's perception of the
firm's competence. If the MIF is able, in a given
interval, to achieve technological advance, then the
TA that it attained during the modification-of-spec-
ifications phase will be increased by 1. This process will be repeated for each time interval in this
phase of contract competition.

Again, the MIF will probably respond to its success or failure in seeking to advance its technical
competence. If the MIF has not had success in advancing its technical competence, it will bring added
resources to bear so that it may do so. The same
rule for increased resource allocation that was described in connection with the modification of specifications will apply here. The increase in resources
will be proportional to the number of time intervals
that have elapsed since the attempts to increase competence were started.

Political Influence

After the contract has crystallized, which corresponds in this model to the time at which the decision is made to develop further competence within
the MIF, the firm begins to try to gain some sort of
political influence to help in winning the contract.
This effort is considered to be successful if it results in an advance in the probability of getting
the contract for each technical level in which the
MIF might find itself.

The same function described previously will be
used here, taking the form:

$$DN(3) = \frac{R_3}{A_3 + (B_3)(R_3)}$$

where $DN(3)$ is again a decision number. R_3 denotes
the quantity of resources allocated for political influence, and A_3 and B_3 are constants. The rule for
determining success will be the same as before.
That is, a random number is chosen from a given pool
and is compared to $DN(3)$. If the random number is

less than or equal to DN(3), then the index of political influence number (PI) is advanced by 1. (This
new non-negative integer has a function similar to
that of the TA. It is an index of political influence achieved by the MIF. Each time the MIF achieves
advances in its political influence, the PI will be
increased by 1.)

Once more the model is designed to take into
account the fact that allocating resources to obtain
political advantage depends on the success that the
MIF achieves through time. If political favor has
not been obtained with a given commitment of resources,
then added resources will be applied. For the model,
the increase will be proportional to the number of
time intervals that have elapsed since attempts to
increase political influence were begun.

Award of Contract

After a number of time intervals have elapsed,
during which the MIF has been expending resources to
develop further competence and to gain political advantage, the award of the contract will be made. If
the MIF is successful, it will add the contract to
its backlog, which will increase and continue to be
the basis for decisions described earlier.

For the purpose of the model, winning a contract
will be treated in a probabilistic way. Since the
probability of winning the contract will depend on
two factors, technical competence and political influence, it can be expressed as the intersection of
the relevant technical-competence and political-in-
fluence factors (See Figure 5). For example, P_{12}
represents the probability of winning the contract,
given that the MIF has attained a PI of 1 and a TA
of 2. Thus, we obtain a matrix of probabilities,
each representing the interaction of technical advances and political influence.

Production

Once a contract is won, it forms part of the
MIF's backlog and represents another need for the

FIGURE 5

Probabilities of Winning the Contract

		TA			
	1	2	3	4	5
1	P_{11}	P_{12}	.	.	.
2	P_{21}	P_{22}	.	.	.
PI 3	.				
4	.				
5	P_{51}	.	.	.	.

allocation of resources, since the DM naturally expects that work will be performed on it. Thus, during each time interval, allocated resources will
produce a reduction in the existing backlog. This
backlog will continue to decline until it is aug-
mented by a new contract award. In the model, the
allocation of resources to production will be considered only implicitly, since it is assumed for
tractability that the backlog is being reduced at a
constant rate. This simplification imposes a limi-
tation on the model, although not a serious one.

Index of Incompetence

Since the DM may be pressured into favoring one
firm over another, regardless of their technical competence in the contract area, it is possible that
the contract winner's performance may require a
"catching up" or compensation for a relatively weak
technical position. An index of this position is
the index of incompetence. The results of this in-
effectiveness may take the form of additional resource needs to meet a specified performance or failures in meeting these specifications. In any case,

there is a weakness found in such a MIF and it is
important that some measure be made of this.

To determine the index, the notion of the TA is
used. It represents the degree of technological
achievement that a firm has been able to attain.   If
a maximum attainable TA can be assumed, then the MIF's
relative competence at the time it receives a contract can be compared with this value.   Specifically,
by subtracting the MIF's attained TA from the maxi-
mal value, we obtain a measure of how ill prepared
the MIF is to carry out the provisions of the contract.   In our model, this may be the result of chance
causes in the award of contract and/or preoccupation
of the MIF with obtaining political influence.

THE SIMULATION

The Program

As the processing of contracts proceeds through
various blocks in the simulation model, the program
computes the backlog of work, total resources allocated, number of rejected contracts, and the number
of completed contracts for each time interval.   Also
recoverable, with a slight modification, is a breakdown of resources into the categories of those allocated respectively to modification of specifications,
to the development of technical competence, and to
the achievement of political influence.

After the designated number of time intervals
have elapsed, means and standard deviations of work
backlog and resource allocation are computed and
printed out, along with total resource allocation,
resources used on rejected contracts, and the ratio
of wasted resources to the total allocated.   An index
of technical incompetence is computed and printed.

Average Backlog

The average backlog, computed for the interval
simulated, gives a quantitative measure of the MIF's
success in winning contracts.

Standard Deviation of Backlog

In addition to the average level of backlog, the MIF must be concerned with the stability of this backlog. That is to say, it will consider a situation with many peaks and valleys in the backlog far less desirable than one where the variation is only slight. The smooth inflow of orders will eliminate costly surges in activity and eliminate the need for various types of curtailments. Thus, the standard deviation, when coupled to the mean backlog, produces a much more significant measure of performance than the average backlog by itself.

Total Resources Allocated

In this model, attention has been focused on three activities: modification of specifications (marketing), development of technical competence, and gaining political influence. Rules were set up for the allocation of resources to these activities.

Total Number of Contracts Won

This is another measure of the effectiveness of the MIF's operation. There is a link between this number and the mean backlog, but this statistic has its own merits.

Ratio of Resources to Contracts Won

A measure of the "efficiency" of resource allocations is the ratio of total resources allocated to number of contracts won. Despite the unusual nature of these allocations, they can be logically tied to the results they produce in a ratio such as this one.

Ratio of Wasted Resources to Total

This is another measure of efficiency. It represents the ratio of resources spent on contracts that were not won to the total resources allocated during the interval simulated. Thus, the higher the ratio, the greater the "waste" of resources on contracts that ultimately were awarded to the competition.

Average Technical Incompetence

During the simulation, a record was kept of the TA that the MIF had developed in the contracts it won. This TA was subtracted from the maximum attainable number (11). The average of these values can be interpreted in several ways. A larger number could indicate that the government was getting a second-rate performance due to the MIF's lack of competence. Or, the MIF might be forced to exceed its original estimates of effort and to seek (and probably gain) additional price concessions from the DM. In either case, an increase in this number will represent a disadvantage to the customer and, eventually, to the MIF itself.

Simulation Parameters

The numerical values in the equations that were used to describe the MIF's activities and its relationships with its environment were, of course, unknown. But, since the purpose of the study was to give clearer meaning to a verbal theory, it was satisfactory to select a set of rather arbitrary parameter values in the assumptions, concentrating on the effects of relative changes in the MIF's circumstances. The discussion that follows identifies the specific values of the program parameters that were previously described in this chapter.

Frequency of Contract Opportunities

In the real world, contract opportunities will appear in some irregular pattern. For the simulation, we assumed that the appearance of contracts was in random fashion and that there was a 50-percent chance of a contract possibility appearing during each time interval.

Allocation of Resources

The initial allocation of resources to the three activities simulated was as follows: modification of specifications, 5 units; development of technical competence, 10 units; political influence, 5 units.

These amounts maintained realistic ratios among these
quantities, since the technical effort is normally
larger than either marketing or influencing, while
the latter two would appear to be about the same.

Probabilities of Success

It will be recalled that the mathematical function used in the model to determine success in effecting a modification of specifications and in advancing
technical competence was dependent on the resources
expended on those activities. In addition, success
was probabilistic in nature. In the simulation, two
sets of probabilities were constructed, with the
higher one representing a more favorable set of circumstances. In other words, with equal resources de-
voted to, say, modification of specifications, one
formula would give a higher probability of success
than the other.

The first set used the values, A = 45, B = 2,
while the second set used the values A = 25, B = 1.
(See page 79.) Thus, the second set represents cor-
respondingly greater probabilities of success (or
advance). In this way, it is possible to analyze
either more or less favorable probabilities in various combinations.

Number of Channels (Contract Capacity)

The number of contracts that the MIF can pursue
simultaneously is a function of its marketing effort
(modification of specifications). In this simulation,
the number of contracts that can be pursued simultaneously is called the number of channels and was set
at 5. Of course, it is possible to vary this number
to measure the change in performance that would result from increased or decreased marketing effort.
Such a change had been incorporated as part of the
model.

Matrix of Probabilities for
Success in Winning Contract

This matrix, whose entries depend on the TA and
the degree of political influence achieved, was kept

constant throughout the simulation. This meant that
the probability of winning two different contracts
with the same TA and PI was the same. Changes might
have been made part of the program without too much
difficulty, but it was felt that enough significant
change could be simulated by varying the three sets
of probabilities mentioned above. This constant set
of probabilities is shown in this chapter.

Number of Time Intervals

The MIF's operation was simulated for a total
of 120 time intervals, each of which represented a
decision-making opportunity. The modification-of-
specifications phase lasted for the first five intervals of a contract opportunity's existence (or until
it was rejected, according to the rules governing
the model). Efforts to achieve technical advance
and political influence occurred simultaneously for
the next five intervals, with the contract award thus
being made ten intervals after the contract opportunity first came into existence.

Size of Contract

Each contract was worth a total of 2,000 units
of work (backlog). If it was won, work began on it
immediately and the amount of its backlog was reduced
by 100 units per interval. A total of twenty intervals was, therefore, needed to complete the contract.
Thus, the simulation did not account for variation
in the production rate and for adjustment of resource
allocation from production to other activities.

Variable Contract Channels

In several cases, when the situation seemed to
warrant it, a set of circumstances (probabilities of
success) was re-run through the computer after changing the number of channels (from five to three).

Variable Probabilities of Success

With two possible probability sets (high and
low) for each of three resource-allocating activities

TABLE 3

Simulation Results for Different Probabilities of Success[a]

	1	2	3	4	5	6	7	8
				Probability of Success				
Specification modification	L	L	L	L	H	H	H	H
Technical advance	L	L	H	H	L	L	H	H
Political influence	L	H	L	H	L	H	L	H
Mean backlog of work	1,370	1,692	1,941	2,195	1,720	1,713	1,693	1,400
Standard deviation of backlog	1,033	1,699	1,505	1,739	1,662	1,246	1,686	1,407
Total resources allocated	8,695	8,035	7,350	6,320	7,925	7,895	6,730	6,860
Total number of contracts won	8	10	13	14	10	10	11	8
Resources allocated per contract won	1,087	804	565	451	793	790	612	858
Ratio of "wasted" resources to total	0.713	0.687	0.565	0.463	0.671	0.709	0.652	0.730
Average technical incompetence	8.07	7.56	6.28	6.66	7.03	6.37	5.21	5.38

[a]L represents the lower set of probabilities for achieving success; H, the higher set.

(modification of specifications, technical competence, and political influence), a total of eight runs was executed and printed out.

Analysis

Effect of Resource Allocation

The LLL situation, column 1 (low probabilities of success for specification modification, for technical advance, and for political influence) can be considered as a beginning point. A move to LLH means that the firm's probability of gaining political influence has increased, while the other two probabilities remain the same. This might be the result of an election that gives greater power to individuals more friendly to the MIF. Or, it might come about when more competent "influencers" are hired by the MIF (retired military officers of the appropriate service branch, for instance). The result, as shown in column 2, is increased success for the firm in its operation backlog, efficiency of resource allocations, and even technical incompetence. The last of these is difficult to understand since political influence would seem to reduce the level of competence that the MIF needs to win a contract. It can only be assumed that the limitations in the model did not allow this factor to exert its expected influence. More will be said about this later.

A move to LHL, with results given in column 3, represents an increase in probability of success in technical advance, while the other two probabilities remain the same. This could be interpreted as an increase in the effectiveness of the firms' engineering and scientific personnel. Again, there is an improvement in all categories over both LLL and LLH. One observes that there was a substantial decrease in the average technical incompetence, which can be explained by greater dependence on real technical progress and less on political influence.

Column 4, showing the results of LHH, gives the largest backlog and most efficient resource utiliza-

tion of the four conditions discussed thus far. One
notes, however, that the average technical incompetence was greater in this case than in LHL. This is,
of course, the effect of greater dependence on political influence.

The effectiveness of decision rules regarding
the allocation of resources can be seen to decline
when increased success is achieved in the modifica-
tion-of-specifications phase of the MIF's operation.
No comment is made on the individual outcomes except
to suggest that the increased probability of success
in marketing, coupled with increased success in the
other two areas, makes a reduction of the former seem
desirable. This is to say that a reduction in search
for contract opportunities will reduce the "spending
of resources," while not harming the firm's chances
of getting contracts. As an illustration, the HHH
conditions were run through the computer a second time
while reducing the number of channels (or sales teams)
from 5 to 3. The results compared with the original
outcomes (column 8) are shown in Table 4. There is

TABLE 4

Comparison of 5-Channel and 3-Channel Simulation

	5 Sales Team	3 Sales Team
Specification modification	H	H
Technical advance	H	H
Political influence	H	H
Mean backlog of work	1,400	1,479
Standard deviation of backlog	1,407	1,085
Total resources allocated	6,860	3,990
Total number of contracts won	8	9
Resources allocated per contract won	858	443
Ratio of "wasted" resources to total	0.730	0.481
Average technical incompetence	5.38	6.41

some evidence that the MIF has an optimal-firm size
determined by its own unique environment. Reducing
the size of the sales effort (5 channels to 3) gives
a larger mean backlog and a more efficient utiliza-
tion of resources.

Efficiency of Resource Use

     There is no universal standard for measuring the
efficiency with which the MIF allocates its resources.
The following results give some indication of the
factors influencing the firm's effectiveness, however.

Relationship of Resources Allocated per Contract Won
and Ratio of "Wasted" Resources to Total. A significant rank correlation exists between these two quantities. It is not, however, perfect, because of the
chance causes that affect the allocation of resources.

Resources Allocated per Contract Won and Average
Backlog. Here, a significant negative-rank correlation was found. This, too, seems to support the notion that there is an optimal size of effort. Simply
pouring in additional resources will not necessarily
provide a proportionate increase in success.

Resources Allocated per Contract Won to Stability.
An attempt was made to discover if there was any relationship between efficiency of resource allocation
and stability of MIF performance. The latter was
determined by the ratio of mean backlog to the standard deviation. There was no significant rank correlation, but a simple testing of the different
simulated conditions in order of stability (Table 5)
suggests an interesting possibility.

     Three of the four most stable situations had
low probabilities of success in modification of specifications, which three of the four least stable had
high probabilities in this activity. The effect on
stability might be explained in terms of unusual
sporadic successes that the sales teams achieve.

TABLE 5

Simulation Outcomes in Order of Stability
(most stable listed first

Order	Probability Conditions
1	HLH
2	LLL
3	LHL
4	LHH
5	HLL
6	HHL
7	LLH
8	HHH

Technical Incompetence

The firm that is best qualified to do the work
may often begin without having too much competence.
The index of technical incompetence was derived to
measure this phenomenon.

Relationship of Average Technical Incompetence to
Mean Backlog. It would be logical to expect a correlation between technical incompetence and backlog,
since the TA has so much importance in determining
which contracts will be pursued and whether the contract will be won. In the simulation, however, no
significant rank correlation between average technical incompetence and mean backlog was found.

Table 6 shows the results, if the simulated
conditions are listed in order of average technical
incompetence, identifying the probability conditions
under which they occurred. These are inconsistent
with the notion that political influence will be the
prime factor in determining the degree of technical
incompetence. One observes that the high and low
probabilities of success in winning political influence are evenly divided between the greater and lesser
technical-incompetence groups. But, it is also

TABLE 6

Simulated Outcomes in Order of Technical
Incompetence

Order	Probability Conditions
1	LLL
2	LLH
3	HLL
4	LHH
5	HLH
6	LHL
7	HHH
8	HHL

evident that the former have the majority of low
specification-modification and technical-advance
probabilities, while the latter have the majority of
high probabilities in these two areas. The model is
obviously structured in such a way as to give greater
weight to the combined effects of these two activities
than to political influence alone.

Relationship of Average Technical Incompetence to
Resources per Contract. There is no significant rank
correlation between technical incompetence and the
efficient use of resources. One might expect that,
in general, the lower the TA at which the contract
is won (and, therefore, the greater the degree of incompetence), the lower the "cost" of the contract.
This is another way of saying that with the lower TA's
one might expect fewer rejections and, thus, a lower
ratio of, say, resources per contract. The interaction and effect of other considerations seem to make
this a far too simple interpretation of the MIF's activity.

Summary

Evaluation of Strategies

The results of changing the use of resources has
been demonstrated for the three areas selected: specification modification, technological advance, and
political influence. (This was done by varying probabilities of success.) Beginning with low probabilities (meaning low effectiveness), the changes in
performance brought about by increased effectiveness
(higher probabilities) were shown. Similarly, beginning with high probabilities for all three, it was
possible to show how single or combined reductions
in effectiveness changed the firm's outcomes.

Measurement of "efficiency" in using the MIF's
resources was illustrated in terms of several ratios
that related the quantity of resources used to the
degree of success in winning contracts. There was
an indication of the existence of an optimal size
for the firm's activity that is dependent on the interaction of the individual probabilities. An illustration was given by a situation in which the firm
gained improved outcomes by reducing the size of its
"marketing" effort.

The analysis of the MIF did not show that any
clear advantage could be gained by advancing technical incompetence. It is logical, therefore, to con-
clude that the firm will normally choose strategies
without the primary emphasis on gaining the largest
possible TA before it begins work on a contract.

Limitations of the Model
and Proposals for Improvement

During the program design and the actual simulation, a number of important components were omitted.
As previously stated, this was the result of bounds
that were accepted for an introductory project of
this sort.

The relationship between technological advance
and modification of specifications is in reality

more closely linked and more interdependent in nature
than that shown in the model. There is a continuing
feedback between the two activities, which goes on
until the contract is actually awarded.

    The contract opportunities appear with far
greater randomness than was incorporated into the
model. Also, the contract sizes are not all the
same, nor is the notion of uniform backlog depletion
very realistic. An improved model might include randomness in size and delivery requirements. Furthermore, the initial TA ought to vary in random fashion,
representing preliminary choices by the DM that match
up, to a greater or lesser degree, with technical
competence attained by the MIF.

    Reduction in backlog, another way of describing
actual performance on the contract, might also vary
randomly, reflecting the uncertainties that are part
of research and development. Then, the occasional
need to allocate additional resources for "catching
up" on contract work can be included as well.

    Negotiation for additional payments on contracts
should be included, particularly if these could be
tied to unfavorable occurrences. For example, if
the firm falls behind in its schedule and needs additional resources to bolster its efforts, the model
would allow a set of allocations to finance this
activity.

    The last two comments lead to the notion of a
closed system in which the quantity of resources
available for allocation is relatively fixed over
some interval. This quantity can be increased by
getting additional funds or by avoiding any unfavorable variations in output. One must also not forget
that one of the strategies important to the MIF is
that of acquiring additional resources from the DM
in the form of plant, facilities, equipment, research
results, etc. A set of strategies directed toward
this end might also be a part of this model.

    Included are only a few of the possible improve-
ments that might be made in the model. Certainly,

the decision rules themselves might be made more complex and realistic. Probabilities might be found
that more accurately represent the MIF's environment.
But the fact remains that the simple model used gives
a significant representation of the MIF's operations
and can form the basis of a more sophisticated and
"practical" version.

5

In this chapter, the theory of the MIF is re-
viewed and summarized. The government's role as a
purchaser of technical products and services is then
reevaluated. Finally, a few proposals for future research are presented.

BEHAVIOR OF THE MIF

The argument that the MIF did not conform to the
behavior patterns associated with existing economic
theories of the firm began with an enumeration of the
decision-making activities that are essential for the
attainment of the goals these theories have promul-
gated. The set of resulting decisions dealt with
quantitative and qualitative aspects of product and
operation. In the classical competitive firm, the
decisions are evaluated in impersonal market places
that reflect judgments that are independent of the
producers. It was shown that the MIF decisions in
the areas of product and operation are made by its
DOD customer. Thus, the conventional opportunities
for "economizing" are not available to the MIF. Instead, it must react to its unique environment by
identifying its own relevant decision-making areas.
And it must understand what the strategic opportunities in these areas are. A theory dealing with this

identification and the resulting possibilities was
then developed in the form of five hypotheses.

The Five Hypotheses

The theory is based on five hypotheses, which
are now repeated in abbreviated form:

1. The MIF will survive only if it allocates
sufficient resources for the development of new technical competence.

2. The MIF selling activity consists of convinc-
ing the DM that a particular technical approach,
based on competence that the firm has been developing,
most satisfactorily meets his goals. If successful,
it means that the firm automatically achieves relative advantages in the competition for the contract.

3. Contract prices are determined through negotiation. This negotiation represents a real opportunity for the MIF to acquire additional resources
because of its favorable strategic position. Furthermore, the negotiation continues until the contract is completed, with additional payments for
changes and additions being the rule rather than the
exception.

4. The MIF has an opportunity to acquire the
equivalent of "free" capital in the form of plant,
facilities, equipment, research results, and so on.
This represents a lucrative goal and motivates the
firm to considerable effort.

5. Top management's principal function is to
win an advantage over competing firms, based on non-
technical considerations. Since the DM's base is
political, this is where he is vulnerable to influence. Gaining such influence may actually be the determining factor in achieving success.

Model Resulting From the Hypotheses

Although the integration of the MIF hypotheses
has been detailed in Chapter 3, an abbreviated

version with schematic representation is given in
this section.

Relation (1) represents the exchange of information between MIF and DM and the influencing of the
latter by the former. It is the "selling" effort
conducted by the MIF team (the retired military man,
the technical specialists, and the sales type). Their
goals are, of course, to persuade the military decision-maker that their own competence and investiga-
tions should form the basis of future contracts and
also to learn the DM's own thoughts in this area,
e.g., the proposals advanced by competing firms.
Thus, there is a two-way flow.

Relation (2) shows engineering-developing competence in accordance with information received from
marketing about the DM's anticipated needs. The marketing group uses the developed competence of the
firm to generate a "sales" effort.

Relation (3) shows the management of the MIF,
acting on information received from the marketing
group, exerting pressures on the DM's political superstructure in order to get a favorable attitude
toward their contract efforts. This takes the form
of "briefing" senators and congressmen representing
the MIF's geographical location on the technical merits of various proposals, as well as detailing the
economic implications of lost contracts. Pressures
by community leaders and labor organizations would
be included here, as would the influence of the retired military men upon their former associates, now
occupying high positions.

Relation (4) shows the MIF management's efforts
to exert pressures on the DM from his political su-
periors. This pressure may, in some cases, take the
form of an overruling of decisions that have already
been made.

Relation (5) indicates management attempts to
get the equivalent of free capital to support its
efforts. The DOD, in the interests of getting a
"good" performance, is willing to provide whatever

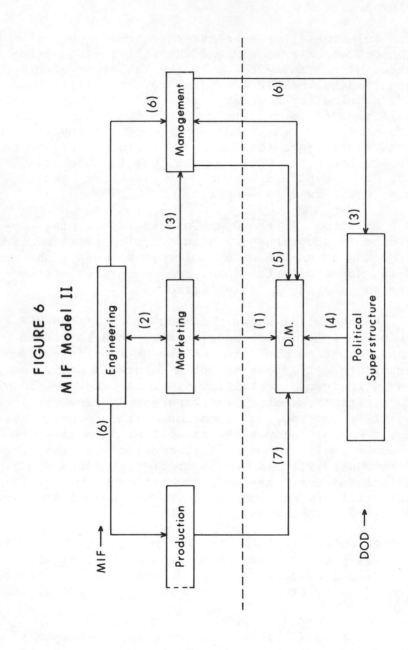

FIGURE 6

MIF Model II

resources and facilities it has available. In order
to broaden its own industrial base, the DOD may provide the MIF with research results of other contracts,
thus giving them a technological competence that
otherwise would have taken considerable time and money
to develop.

Relation (6) shows that the MIF's performance on
the contract will be largely determined by the technical competence that the firm has been able to develop. Lack of success in this direction will
probably mean increased pressure on management to
get more money for the contract. In any case, the
strategy of the MIF is the "expansion" of its contract in the form of changes and added complexity.
This promotes negotiations for increased money payments by the DM.

Relation (7) shows that delivery (meaning total
performance) may have some significance in determining
how the MIF will fare in future competition. But
this is not an important factor, except that it under-
scores the very close mutual dependency of the MIF
and the DM. Their interests are so similar that the
use of actual contract performance as a control device becomes virtually impossible. Judging whether
a contract could have been fulfilled more effectively
in such areas of uncertainty would be a formidable
task. Coupled with the personal interests of the DM
in maintaining his image of competence in the award
of contracts, the total effect is a situation in
which use of basic economic criteria is rendered almost totally inoperative.

Results of the Simulation

The simulation of the MIF's behavior was included to suggest a method of understanding its performance and in this way to further illustrate its
operating characteristics. One usually turns to the
conventional accounting model, but this has been demonstrated to be an inappropriate device for the MIF.
In particular, the simulation has used the following
dimensions for measuring the firm's performance:
mean backlog and standard deviation; efficiency of

resources usage, stated in terms of resources/con-
tract or percentage of total resources expended un-
successfully; and technical incompetence, defined as
the distance that separated the MIF from maximum possible technological advance at the time the contract
was awarded.

Summary and Conclusions

In developing the first hypothesis, the MIF's
principal product was identified as "technical competence," but it was also indicated that developing
such competence was only a part of the success-pro-
ducing activity required of the MIF. As a matter of
fact, it was pointed out several times that there
need be no positive correlation between a firm's
technical performance in the past and its success in
getting future awards (see Chapter 2).

What the MIF is left to do is weigh the desir-
ability of various courses of action. Thus, the
choice between having a newly retired admiral and a
newly graduated Ph.D. is an excellent example of decision-making in the MIF's environment. The Ph.D.
may contribute to the MIF's technological advance,
but the military officer may strengthen the DM's image of the firm's reliability. This issue leads to
two observations:

First, the MIF has the same suboptimization
problem that the civilian firm has, but its goals are
the singular product of its own special environment.*
The goals themselves represent components of a total
ability to satisfy the customer. The MIF's management must define a balanced effort toward organizational goal achievement in terms of how well it is
able to develop a total competence in its dealings
with the DM. Thus, the classic civilian firm seeks
to suboptimize such objectives as innovation,

───────────────

*Suboptimization is the process of optimizing one
set of activities with respect to a certain goal, at
the expense of an optimal level of performance elsewhere or in the system considered as a totality.

productivity, return on investments, divided payments, share of markets, development of new resources, etc., all of which represent areas of need and opportunity essential for survival and continuing profitability in the market place.

Second, the MIF has been shown to have the following goals: to supply the DOD with ideas for new products, these being the result of its continuous development of new technical competence; to promote these ideas and to influence the DM to originate contracts that will coincide with its own technical competence and thus increase the likelihood of success in getting new business; to develop an image of responsibility as a performer and of influence in the DOD's political superstructure; to make the DM's perception of the MIF one of high dependence and reliability and to minimize the probability that a contract will be lost to a competitor because of political pressures from any source; to take advantage of the unique relationship between the DOD and the MIF by drawing on various resources made available by the former, including the results of research that will provide entry into new fields; and to expand the revenue from contracts by increasing the complexity of the products and thus justifying additional costs, additional payments, and additional budget requests.

FIRMS SIMILAR TO THE MIF

One might ask whether there are any firms in the civilian economy that have attributes similar to those of the MIF and whether the theory that has been developed here might not apply to them as well. There are three types of non-military industrial activities that might be tested for this similarity. They have, at least superficially, some important features in common with the MIF.

One can consider civilian firms that sell to local and state governments--for example, the contractor

who builds schools and other public structures. He
is usually dealing with some governmental department
roughly analogous to the DOD. There is no reason to
suspect that this contracting agency is any less
concerned with the reliability of its performers, in
the sense that we have used this word, than is the
DOD.

Manufacturers of products that are sold nationally by mail-order houses can also be considered.
Here is a situation in which the customer may have
considerable control over the supplier. He might
furnish capital, specify the nature of the product,
determine how it is to be made, oversee the cost system, make rulings about the allowable profit, etc.
Certainly, this suggests a relationship similar to
that of the DOD and the MIF.

Finally, there are civilian firms producing
highly technical products for the civilian market.
One example would be the division of an electrical
company that manufactures large turbines for special
installations, each one being unique and requiring a
new design. This is a situation where technical complexity is an important factor.

Although all three of these activities have certain points in common with the MIF, they also have
sharp differences. These differences make it impossible to apply the theory of the MIF to them.

Each of the above firms makes a product that is
salable in a number of market places or to a variety
of customers. The contractor may engage in private
construction; the vacuum cleaner made for the mail-
order house may be offered, often with only a change
in name plate, to many other vendors; the turbine
manufacturer may sell to new installations all over
the world. But General Dynamics cannot offer to sell
a Polaris submarine, produced in its yards in Con-
necticut, to a foreign country. Therefore, the dependency on and the control of the buyer is multiplied
in a way that, for the MIF, produces a fundamental
and qualitative difference.

The products of the above firms are better understood than those of the MIF and, consequently,
are more sensitive to the evaluation of the market
place. The contractor bids on a highly specific set
of blueprints and will go to prison if his work does
not match them. The mail-order house will specify
the nature of the product on the basis of its market
research and will certainly be able to determine
whether the technical performance is exactly what it
should be. The turbine customer will demand certain
performance characteristics and will generally have
his own technical people cooperate with the manufacturer's engineering department during the actual design and building of the equipment.

There is less of a continuing dependency of customer on supplier in the above three activities than
in the case of the MIF. Even if one considers a situation in which one civilian firm were to build a
technologically advanced product for another civilian
firm, with no possibilities of selling it again or
to someone else, as soon as the transaction is completed, the relationship between the two firms is
ended. But the MIF and the DOD are united by a joint
expectation of a continuing partnership in the development of a highly technical product that cannot be
sold in any other market. The city can find other
contractors, and the contractors can find other customers. The mail-order house will find other suppliers if it is not satisfied with current performance.
As for the DOD and the MIF, each has no place else
to go. The result has been a mutation of the classic
supplier-customer relationship.

With no market alternative, with the customer's
great dependence on it for technological advance, and
with a mutual interest in expanding the activities
of the military-industrial complex, it is clear that
the MIF has no counterpart in the civilian world.
Furthermore, because it has become accustomed to this
unique environment, it may be said that a military
department of a largely non-military firm would, in
effect, be destroying itself if it decided to aban-
don its dealings with the DOD and enter the civilian
market.

SIMILARITIES TO THE DM-MIF
RELATIONSHIP

It is possible to develop striking parallels between the DM-MIF relationship and the situation existing in large decentralized civilian firms. Consider, for example, Henry H. Albers' description of a large multidivisional civilian firm, based on Peter Drucker's famous study of the General Motors Corporation:

> Central management formulates top-corporate operating and financial policy. It establishes a broad framework within which the divisions are expected to operate. It plans the total manufacturing program and determines the amount of capital that is allocated to each division. It coordinates the activities of the divisions and provides a unity of purpose throughout the corporation . . .
>
> In addition to the function of overall corporate planning, central management has retained decision-making prerogatives for certain aspects of division operations. For example, it assigns minimum production quotas and sets a price range for major product lines. Contract negotiation with unions is essentially a top-management affair, and the appointment of top division executives is subject to central-management veto. Centrally determined standards and procedures are used in a number of areas, such as accounting and position classification for salaried employees.[1]

The ease with which the various aspects of the DOD-MIF association could be matched up with this set of activities is quite evident.

IMPROVING GOVERNMENT ACQUISITION

The Present Method of Government
Contracting

The comparison of the MIF with a typical Soviet
enterprise is included for a definite purpose, relating to the general problem of government contracting
for services of a highly technical nature. It was
found that adherence to the trappings of free enterprise does not produce very effective results. The
MIF's environment creates behavior patterns directed
at circumventing imposed and unnecessary obstacles
to the enterprise's success or efforts to improve the
firm's position without increasing the "value" of its
output.

Specifically, in the case of the MIF, a number
of questions can be raised. How much does competition for contracts cost, and what is the technological gain? The large number of highly qualified
engineers and scientists who are engaged in preparing
and writing proposals represents a high alternative
cost since many technical man-hours are expended on
unsuccessful campaigns. Can the technical advantage
gained through competition justify this expenditure
of one of society's most needed talents? Is there,
in fact, any technical advantage accruing to the customer from a competition that is permeated with highly
subjective factors? Is it not possible that the considerable duplication involved in parallel efforts
by several firms actually causes inefficiency in technical advance? The lack of coordination, on a national scale, must mean that precious and scarce
human resources are being used inefficiently. While
not all of the resources used in the preparation of
unsuccessful proposals should be considered a total
loss, the size and intensity of such activity in the
MIF leads to the conclusion that the duplication here
is not justifiable.

The highly subjective nature of the relationships involved in the MIF's functioning, coupled with
the imbalance between the DM's and the firm's

competence in understanding proposals, lead to the
conclusion that the basis for awarding contracts can
not be defended on any rational grounds. The above
questions, if answered honestly, suggest a more appropriate scheme for handling government purchase of
highly technical products and services. While there
is little experience, as yet, on which to draw for
illustration of such a system, the foundation can be
deduced without much difficulty from the results of
the simulation.

Proposal for an Improved Method

Any proposal for an improved method of government contracting for highly technical services must
be based on the recognition of at least five phases
of this activity: technical proposal development,
assignment of priorities to competing projects, con-
stitutional authority for the expenditure of public
funds, award of the contract to do the approved work
to some enterprise or organization, and control and
evaluation of performance on awarded contracts.

Technical Proposal Development

The understanding of a proposal and the evaluation of competing proposals are tasks that can only
be performed by people who are qualified and objective. Even more basic is a definition of problem
areas or selection of those projects or products that
need to be worked on and developed. These activities
should be separated since the interests of the former
are not always best served by the demands of the latter. One approach that comes to mind is that of the
academy, a full-time congress of scientists and engineers that will function as a goal-setting, problem-
defining, and specification-writing group. The
members would be government employees, but with great
autonomy in matters of staffing and compensation.
They could be expected to translate the potential of
technical achievements into useful programs. They
could continually revise our list of national goals
in accordance with perceived needs and rapidly developing technological competence.

Assignment of Priorities

One can easily see that the problem of selecting
one program over another or of determining how much
money shall be spent on parts of various programs is
a decision that should not be left to the scientific
academy. One needs a second entity to make these decisions. Certainly, the scientists will be part of
this group, but there are a number of other parties
who need representation. The political community,
consisting of elected and appointed officials, should
have a voice. So should the labor unions, industrial
associations, farmers, urban groups, and other major
socio-economic components of society. Their principal function will be to recommend the priorities that
should be assigned to the programs developed by the
academy. They would do this after the scientific
members of the group translated the technical efforts
of individual programs into utilitarian or social
values.

Allocation of Funds

The authority to spend public money belongs, of
course, to the U.S. Congress. There is no need to
change this situation in contracting for technical
work, but some sort of formal recognition should be
given to the assigned priorities.

Award of Contracts

Organizations that will actually perform the
contract work should clearly be recognized as "satel-
lite" firms of the government. Private ownership
should be eliminated and their organizational structure should correspond to the realities of the environment in which they function. There would be no
"top management" in the conventional sense, and no
sales teams or marketing organization. The highest
level of management would be a program manager, and,
unless there was an advantage to coalitions of several such programs, the MIF size would be determined
by the requirements of the specific program to which
it had been assigned. The word "firm" here is used
in quite a different way. More will be said about
this later.

Control and Evaluation of Performance

This function would logically be assigned to the academy. Part of its responsibility would be the review of performance, recognition of and action on superior and inferior performances, plus a continuing evaluation and redesign of the entire contracting system.

PROPOSALS FOR FUTURE RESEARCH

Role of Organized Labor

Although the employees of the MIF (usually organized) have been described as obviously interested in the firm's continued success and as a force that may react politically to any signs of adverse decisions on the part of their elected representatives, the role of organized labor should be more thoroughly explored. The reasons for their support of defense-procurement institutions, with disadvantages of which they must surely be aware, might be investigated.

Extent of Political Influence

The MIF is active, through a variety of agents, in exerting influence on the DOD decision-makers to favor one proposed weapons system over another. But influence is a force that is not easily bounded. How far does it penetrate beyond the mere selection of products? Can its effects be found in the development of the policies that assure the MIF's continued existence in foreign affairs, in national priorities, and the like? There has been much speculation but apparently very little serious investigation here. The significance is certainly enormous.

The Scientific Academy

A large number of administrative questions concerning the academy must be answered. What should be its size and composition? Would membership be permanent? How would compensation be determined? Authority and accountability must be clearly defined.

A system of information collection, classification sorting, storage, analysis, matching, and recov-
ery must be designed. The literature of scientific
and engineering societies has many articles that describe the problem of doing this on a company-wide
basis. The system proposed here will be, at least,
a nation-wide one. Its purpose is to provide the
foundation for the academy's principal functions.
The information will be used to control current performance and serve as the springboard for new contracts.

Three aspects of writing program proposals deserve considerable attention. One, of course, is the
decision-making process that will be used to define
problems or goals for the contracts. A second should
deal with the optimal size of a program. The third
involves the format or content of a program proposal
and would be concerned with the degree of detail that
ought to be included.

The Priorities Group

The same administrative questions as those asked
about the scientific academy need answers here. A
set of rules for decision-making by this group should
be developed; they ought to be based on the existing
knowledge of group behavior coupled with predetermined
rational guidelines.

The Firm

A new notion of organization needs to be developed. The changing nature of the tasks that will be
assigned to these associations of highly skilled individuals suggest a strong need for much greater flexibility in their formation and operation. The 19th-
century basis of current firms should not be accepted
even as a point of departure for the design of these
new entities. Grouping people in single physical lo-
cations might not be necessary. Modern communication
methods make it possible to link connected activities
that are widespread geographically, providing that
material transfer is not an important element. Some
of the advances in modular construction of production

systems might be applied to what is essentially
"brain" work. Whatever production facilities are
needed should have the same kind of flexibility one
associates with numerically controlled machine tools.
This approach would have the additional advantage of
reducing regional pressures on elected representatives
to fight for government contracts.

The design of an organization needed to work on
a contract requires a new approach to the inventory
of skills, particularly human ones. A valid method
of profiling individual competences and matching them
up with task requirement is needed. Current practices,
which combine formal education with previous project
involvement, are totally unsatisfactory. This is a
two-way problem. It will be necessary to translate
the contract into a set of human specifications.
Then, one must be able to evaluate (or measure) an
engineer or scientist in these same dimensions. A
number of studies dealing with the transferability
of individuals from military work to other employment give clear evidence that long-established practices of staffing in technical organizations are
unreliable.

Prospects

It seems likely that if such changes as the
above are made in the organizations that provide engineering and technical services to the government,
they will lead in the move toward new, innovative
organizational firms in the society at large.

NOTE

1. Henry H. Albers, <u>Principles of Organization
and Management</u> (New York: John Wiley and Sons, Inc.,
1965), pp. 170-71.

APPENDIX

A

COMPARISON
OF THE MIF
WITH
THE
SOVIET FIRM

This analysis is founded on a study of the Soviet economy made before the major changes of 1965, when the Sovnarkhoz was replaced by another system of central administration. This change, however, does not seem likely, by itself, to produce significant modifications in those characteristics of the Soviet firm's operation that are used as the basis of a comparison with the MIF.

STRUCTURE AND RELATIONSHIPS

In Chapter 2, a graphic structure of the MIF was presented in order to illustrate an important difference between it and the civilian firm. It is reproduced in Appendix Figure A.1, with slight modification, so that it might serve as the basis of a claim that there is similarity between the MIF's operating environment and the one in which the typical Soviet firm functions. The point is that the structure differs radically from that of the typical civilian firm in the location of the principal interface

FIGURE A.1

Structure of the MIF

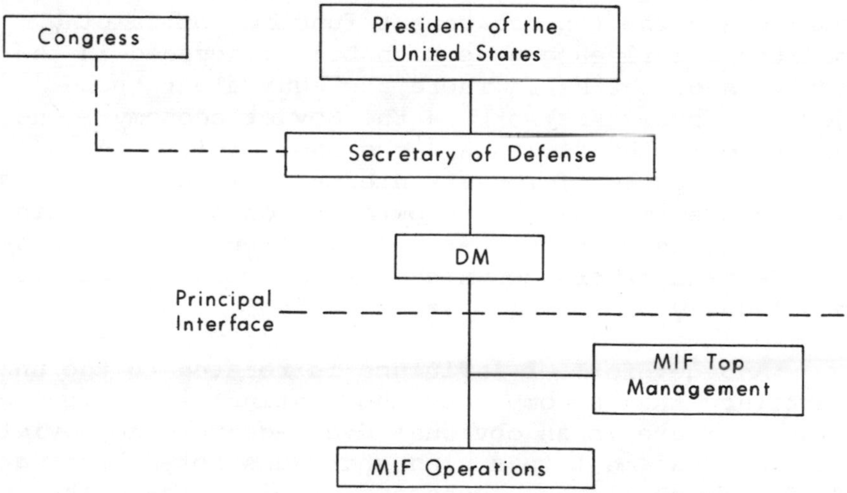

between the firm and the outside world. The civilian
firm might be diagrammed as in Appendix Figure A.2.
In the civilian firm, the interface exists between
its operations (representing a complex set of decisions) and an impersonal market that evaluates
these decisions in the degree of acceptance it awards
to the firm's product. But the MIF's principal interface is with a bureaucratic entity that does not
have the same characteristics as the economic market
place.

A simplified version of the interface for the
Soviet firm[1] is shown in Appendix Figure A.3. Note
that the principal interface here is of the same
nature as the one that confronts the MIF. Although
the enterprise presumably functions to satisfy the
needs of a market that has, superficially, the same
characteristics as those of the U.S. civilian firm,
its principal responsibilities and relationships
involve the same kind of bureaucratic structure as
that encountered by the MIF. Appendix Table A.1 is
presented as a means of comparing the mutations that
this singular interface develops.

Influence

The role of the retired military officer in
developing contacts with the appropriate decision-
makers and the top management function of gaining
political influence have both been discussed in the
analysis of the MIF. There are equivalent "subjective forces" at work in the Soviet economy. One
of these in the "tolkach," the name applied to an
agent who pushes for the "interests of the enterprise
in such matters as the procurement of supplies," in
which use is made "of personal influence for obtaining certain favors to which a firm or individual is
not legally or formally entitled."[2]

Another form of influence is related to the uncertainty that accompanies the setting of enterprise
plans. There is an obvious advantage for the Soviet
firm's management in a plan that does not present a
difficult challenge, because this will assure the
bonus and recognition that constitute their principal
goals. The manager, in his role of participant in

FIGURE A.2
Structure of the Civilian Firm

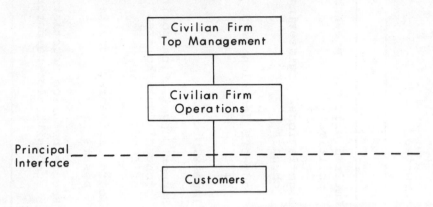

FIGURE A.3
Structure of the Soviet Enterprise

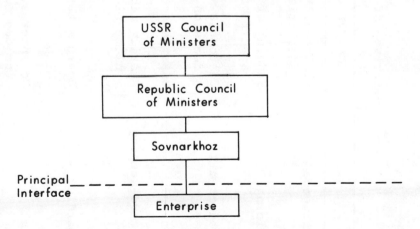

APPENDIX TABLE A.1

Comparison of the MIF with Soviet Enterprise

Comparison Basis	USSR	MIF
1. Influence	"Tolkach," interaction of personalities	Retired military, pressures on political figures
2. Pricing	Padding of cost plans, new specifications	Negotiations, engineering changes
3. Product mix	Customers must accept firm's decision	Trade-off decisions made by MIF
4. Control	Unsatisfactory	Impossible
5. Record-keeping	Justify resource demands, simulate plan fulfillment	Support negotiating position, conceal "unauthorized" use of funds
6. Hoarding	Hoard materials, fixed assets	Hoard engineers, acquired assets
7. Risk	No interest charge on capital, no depreciation charge on uninstalled equipment	Reduce by price negotiation, acquisition of resources

plan formulation, has an opportunity to influence the
final result in a favorable way. Barry M. Richman
describes the possibilities associated with the situation as follows:

> For example, one Soviet source reflects the
> significance of subjective forces in plan-
> ning decisions by citing an actual case in-
> volving a newly appointed shipbuilding
> enterprise director, named Mairov;

> "Not for nothing do they say at the ship-
> yard that Mairov began to increase the
> per cent of plan fulfillment before he
> reached Astrakhan. Indeed, as soon as he
> was appointed the annual plan was reduced
> and the enterprise's output was revalued
> at higher prices. This cost the state
> much, but the enterprise climbed to a
> leading place in plan fulfillment."[3]

Pricing

The MIF uses its great technical and operational
advantages in the negotiation for a contract price to
exact a sum that protects it against the uncertainties
involved in its performance. These advantages stem
from the familiarity it has with its own technical
developments and its day-to-day production activities
--a familiarity not shared by the DM. The Soviet firm
has, in equivalent situations, the same kind of opportunity. Again, Richman comments on this situation.

> Prices are inflated by padding related cost-
> plus estimates, and this often enables man-
> agement to derive excess resources, as well
> as easy success indicator targets. Evidence
> suggests that the emphasis on cost reduc-
> tion as a key success indicator has inten-
> sified management's efforts to engage in
> pricing distortions. Price inflation is
> most prevalent at enterprises producing un-
> standardized output, new products, and where
> specification changes in products are often
> undertaken.[4]

Product Mix

It is important to recall the MIF's version of
the product-mix problem: the tradeoffs that must be
made among time, quality, and cost. Only the MIF has
the competence to originate and implement these decisions, and it is not likely that its own interests
will be treated as secondary in its evaluation of
alternative courses of action. The following comment
by Richman illustrates the similarity of the Soviet
firm on this point:

> In its product choices the enterprise has
> no incentive to satisfy consumer require-
> ments or demand, but every incentive to
> fulfill its aggregate success indicators.
> If machine A is more productive and/or
> durable than machine B, but for various
> reasons machine B is more beneficial for
> success indicator performance, the en-
> terprise may substitute more production
> of B in place of A. The same would be
> true for material or shoe type x and ma-
> terial or shoe type y, where x is in
> greater demand, but y is more beneficial.[5]

Control

If we define control as an activity that is
concerned with seeing how well actual performance
corresponds with plans, immediate difficulty is
encountered in trying to apply it to the MIF. The
uncertainties involved make it difficult to compare
plans and performance unambiguously. Furthermore,
any sort of objective evaluation of progress on a
contract is nearly impossible because of the complexity of the program and the limited resources of
the evaluation. The Soviet firm is in a similar
position, primarily because of the latter factor.
In an attempt to remedy this situation, the form of
administration was changed from the national ministry
to regional councils. "Administration had shifted
from organization by type of product to organization
by geographic region."[6] According to David Granick,
"One may interpret this desire for closer contact as

simply representing an effort to improve the quality
of higher-level decisions. But this strikes me as a
naive interpretation. Far more important, we have
here an effort to regain central control."[7]

Record-Keeping

In the MIF, it was suggested that records may
serve two purposes: to form the basis of proposals
for prices on new contracts and to conform with a
concept of free enterprise that the DM has decided
upon as the milieu for its operation. The Soviet
firm, functioning in an artificial environment, will
also use its records to further its own aims. One
often hears the word "simulation" used in describing
Soviet managerial activity.

To illustrate the activity of the Soviet firm,
the Webster definition of simulation is used--"assumption of the appearance of, without the reality."
Simulation becomes possible when the controller or
evaluator becomes relatively less competent in the
area of performance than the performer. The term is
frequently encountered in Berliner's study of Soviet
industrial management.

> Every Soviet manager wishes to fulfill his
> plan if he can. But in a system character-
> ized by high targets and uncertain sources
> of supply he is constantly confronted with
> the threat of failure . . . Simulation is
> a normal recourse of a manager in the nor-
> mal situation of impending underfulfill-
> ment.[8]

In the Soviet Union, the artificial method of
evaluating performance makes simulation desirable.
The evaluation of the factory manager's performance
by the national ministry or regional council is
followed by an evaluation of the ministry or council's performance by higher officials. As the distance from the operating level increases, there is
a decrease in the ability to evaluate the performance
of the factory manager. Even the establishment of a
special agency for this purpose might not be very
helpful.

Hoarding

There is at least one example of hoarding in the
MIF. In developing competence, the presence of high-
quality engineers and special facilities makes the
perception of the MIF by the DM much more favorable
and increases the likelihood of a contract award.
Thus, the MIF hoards technical personnel. The Soviet
firm will also benefit from hoarding, since an ex-
cess of plant and equipment can be considered a
safety factor in the effort to attain enterprise
plans. Richman observes, on Soviet enterprises, that
"many plants are evidently successful in hoarding
and maintaining overabundant quantities of fixed
assets."[9]

Risk

The reduction in risk for the MIF occurs through
negotiation for the original contract price, through
additional payments for engineering changes, and the
availability of government-owned resources. There
is an obvious motivation for the DM to make the MIF
a satisfied and willing participant in military contracting. The MIF accepts the reduced risk as part
of a mutual-responsibility system involving it and
the DM. A Soviet enterprise reduces its risk in
fulfilling plans and targets by hoarding productive
assets, such as equipment and supplies and working
capital.

Summary

It must be admitted that among the forces that
influence the Soviet firm there are several that do
not have identical counterparts in the MIF's operations. As examples, there is the assignment of un-
realistic targets for the Soviet firm and the per-
vasive shortage of resources. But this does not
weaken the claim that, in both cases, the systems
are not regulated by a free market. Operating in
bureaucratic environments, the Soviet firm and the
MIF will resort to the use of influence, self-serving
pricing strategies, a product mix that is in the
firm's best interests, overcoming controls, simulation

in record-keeping, hoarding of resources, and the
minimization of risk.

NOTES

1. The sources used for the anlaysis of the
Soviet firms are David Granick, <u>The Red Executive</u>
(Garden City, N.Y.: Doubleday and Co., Inc., 1960);
Joseph S. Berliner, <u>Factory and Manager in the USSR</u>
(Cambridge, Mass.: Harvard University Press, 1957);
and Barry M. Richman, <u>Soviet Management: With Sig-
nificant American Comparisons</u> (Englewood Cliffs,
N.J.: Prentice-Hall, Inc., 1965).

2. Berliner, <u>op. cit.</u>, p. 210.

3. Richman, <u>op. cit.</u>, p. 162.

4. <u>Ibid.</u>, p. 158.

5. <u>Ibid.</u>, p. 164.

6. Granick, <u>op. cit.</u>, p. 162.

7. <u>Ibid.</u>, p. 163.

8. Berliner, <u>op. cit.</u>, p. 114.

9. Richman, <u>op. cit.</u>, p. 153.

B

FLOW CHART

FOR

THE

SIMULATION

PROGRAM

Computational Procedure

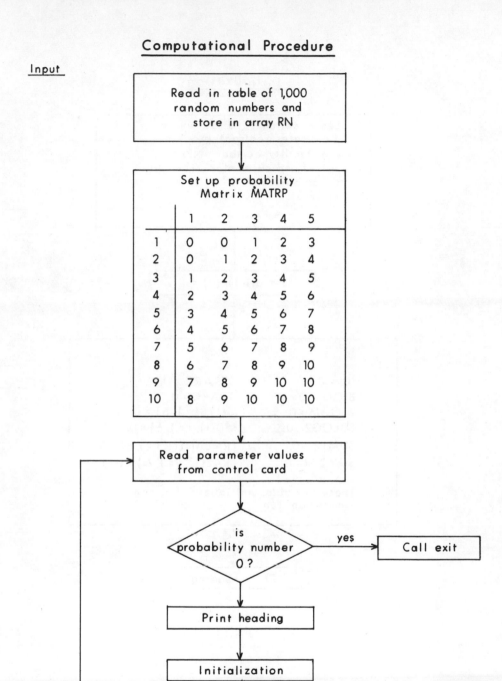

Initialization

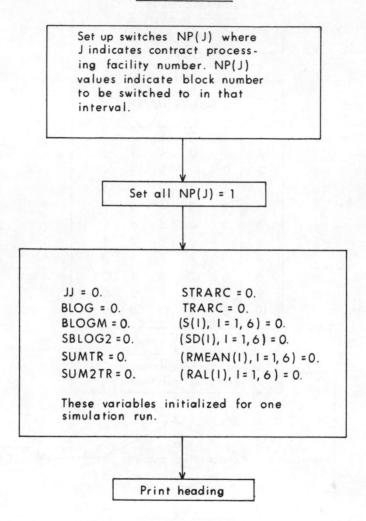

Set up switches NP(J) where J indicates contract processing facility number. NP(J) values indicate block number to be switched to in that interval.

Set all NP(J) = 1

JJ = 0.   STRARC = 0.
BLOG = 0.   TRARC = 0.
BLOGM = 0.   (S(I), I = 1, 6) = 0.
SBLOG2 = 0.   (SD(I), I = 1, 6) = 0.
SUMTR = 0.   (RMEAN(I), I = 1, 6) = 0.
SUM2TR = 0.   (RAL(I), I = 1, 6) = 0.

These variables initialized for one simulation run.

Print heading

For the simulation, the program was structured as follows. The number of time intervals and the capacity of the firm having been read in as variables, the program scans through each time interval starting with 1. It scans each facility in turn up to the number of facilities read in as variable JCAP. Each facility is occupied by a contract in some stage of processing or by a contract possibility. These stages consist of four main program blocks. Each contract has an NP(J) number that is set to the number of the program block it is to go to for the coming time interval. At the end of processing for that interval, the number is reset to indicate the contract's next stage to completion. Therefore, although the flow of the program is from facility to facility in the same time interval, the flow of the processing of each contract through time proceeds in an orderly manner through the blocks.

The following flow charts, that of the general plan of the main program and those of the four blocks, show how this is done.

Main Program Flow Chart

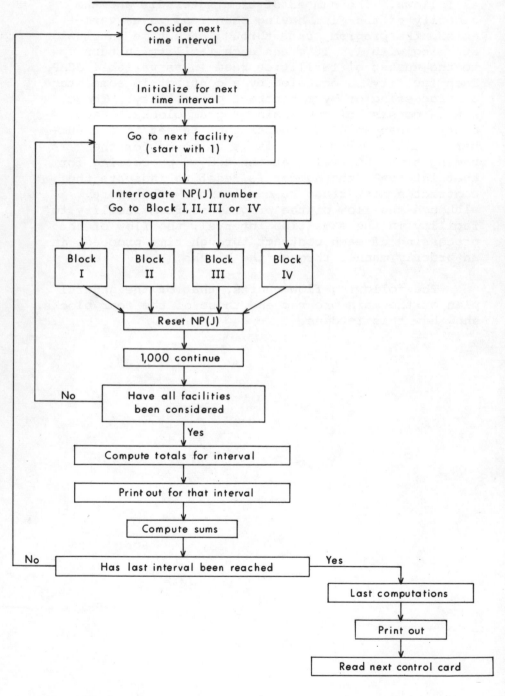

Block I--Contract Possibility Exists

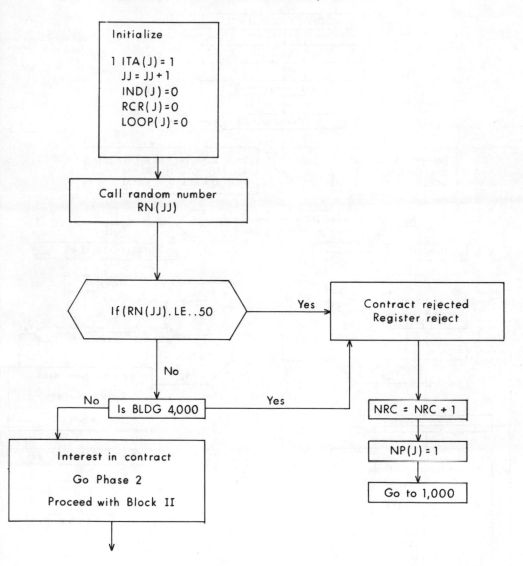

Initialize

1 ITA(J) = 1
 JJ = JJ + 1
 IND(J) = 0
 RCR(J) = 0
 LOOP(J) = 0

Call random number
RN(JJ)

If (RN(JJ).LE..50

Yes

Contract rejected
Register reject

No

Is BLDG 4,000

Yes

No

Interest in contract

Go Phase 2

Proceed with Block II

NRC = NRC + 1

NP(J) = 1

Go to 1,000

Block II-- Contract Under Consideration

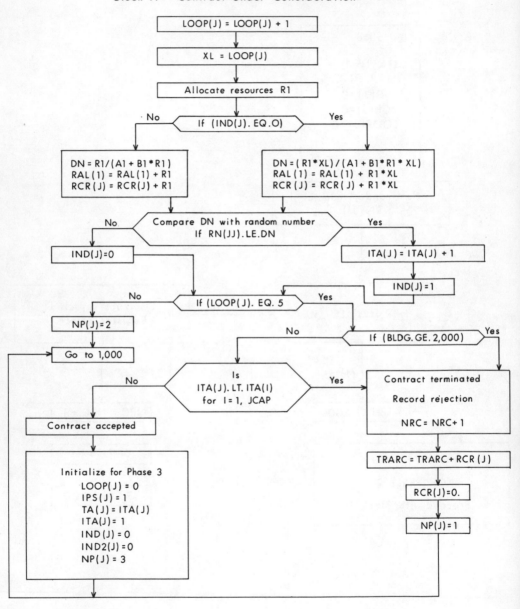

Block III-- Determine Whether Contract Is Won

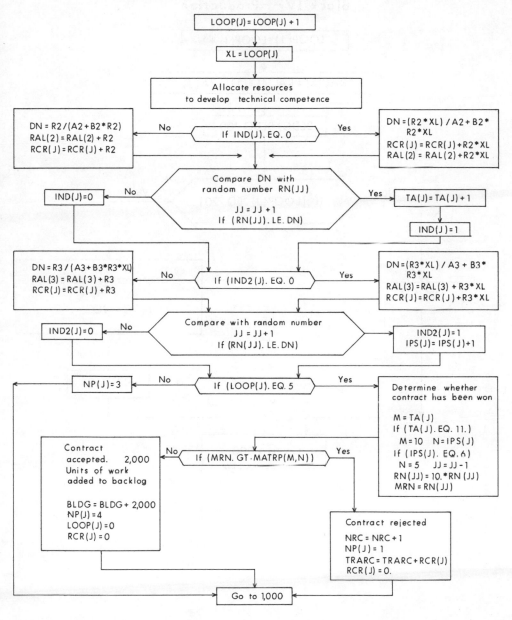

LOOP(J) = LOOP(J) + 1

XL = LOOP(J)

Allocate resources
to develop technical competence

If IND(J). EQ. 0

No →
DN = R2 / (A2 + B2*R2)
RAL(2) = RAL(2) + R2
RCR(J) = RCR(J) + R2

Yes →
DN = (R2*XL) / A2 + B2*
R2*XL
RCR(J) = RCR(J) + R2*XL
RAL(2) = RAL(2) + R2*XL

Compare DN with
random number RN(JJ)
JJ = JJ + 1
If (RN(JJ). LE. DN)

No → IND(J) = 0

Yes → TA(J) = TA(J) + 1

IND(J) = 1

If (IND2(J). EQ. 0

No →
DN = R3 / (A3 + B3*R3*XL)
RAL(3) = RAL(3) + R3
RCR(J) = RCR(J) + R3

Yes →
DN = (R3*XL) / A3 + B3*
R3*XL
RAL(3) = RAL(3) + R3*XL
RCR(J) = RCR(J) + R3*XL

Compare with random number
JJ = JJ + 1
If (RN(JJ). LE. DN)

No → IND2(J) = 0

IND2(J) = 1
IPS(J) = IPS(J) + 1

If (LOOP(J). EQ. 5

No → NP(J) = 3

Yes →
Determine whether
contract has been won

M = TA(J)
If (TA(J). EQ. 11.)
  M = 10 N = IPS(J)
If (IPS(J). EQ. 6)
  N = 5 JJ = JJ - 1
RN(JJ) = 10.*RN (JJ)
MRN = RN(JJ)

If (MRN. GT. MATRP(M,N))

No →
Contract
accepted. 2,000
Units of work
added to backlog

BLDG = BLDG + 2,000
NP(J) = 4
LOOP(J) = 0
RCR(J) = 0

Yes →
Contract rejected

NRC = NRC + 1
NP(J) = 1
TRARC = TRARC + RCR(J)
RCR(J) = 0.

Go to 1,000

Block IV -- Production

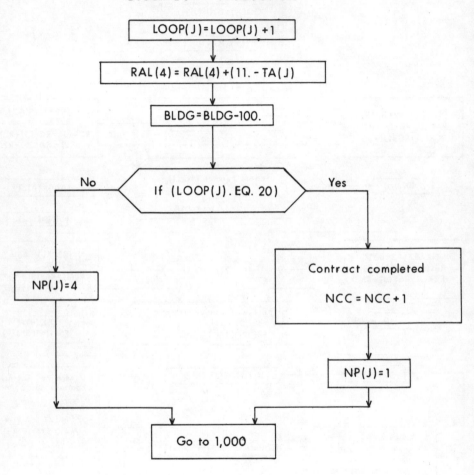

LOOP(J)=LOOP(J)+1

RAL(4)=RAL(4)+(11.-TA(J)

BLDG=BLDG-100.

No — If (LOOP(J).EQ. 20) — Yes

NP(J)=4

Contract completed

NCC = NCC+1

NP(J)=1

Go to 1,000

BIBLIOGRAPHY

BOOKS

Churchman, C. West. Prediction and Optimal Decision. Englewood Cliffs, N.J.: Prentice-Hall, Inc., 1961.

Cole, Arthur H. "An Approach to the Study of Entrepreneurship." Enterprise and Secular Change. Edited by F. C. Lane and J. C. Riemersma. Homewood, Ill.: Richard D. Irwin, Inc., 1953.

Cyert, Richard M., and March, James G. A Behavioral Theory of the Firm. Englewood Cliffs, N.J.: Prentice-Hall, Inc., 1963.

Dean, Joel. Managerial Economics. Englewood Cliffs, N.J.: Prentice-Hall, Inc., 1951.

McGuire, Joseph W. Theories of Business Behavior. Englewood Cliffs, N.J.: Prentice-Hall, Inc., 1964.

Peck, Merton J., and Scherer, Frederick M. The Weapons Acquisition Process: An Economic Analysis. Cambridge, Mass.: Graduate School of Business Administration, Harvard University, 1962.

Scherer, Frederick M. The Weapons Acquisition Process: Economic Incentives. Cambridge, Mass.: Graduate School of Business Administration, Harvard University, 1964.

Williamson, Oliver E. The Economics of Discretionary Behavior: Managerial Objectives in a Theory of the Firm. Englewood Cliffs, N.J.: Prentice-Hall, Inc., 1964.

GOVERNMENT PUBLICATIONS

Gilmore, John S., and Coddington, Dean C. Defense Industry Diversification. U.S. Arms Control and Disarmament Agency Publication No. 30. Washington, D.C.: Government Printing Office, January, 1966.

McDonagh, James J., and Zimmerman, Steven M. "A
     Program for Civilian Diversification of the
     Airframe Industry." Convertibility of Space
     and Defense Resources to Civilian Needs: A
     Search for New Employment Potentials. Vol. II.
     Compiled for U.S. Senate, Subcommittee on Em-
     ployment and Manpower of the Committee on Labor
     and Public Welfare. Washington, D.C.: Govern-
     ment Printing Office, 1964.

U.S. Bureau of the Census. Statistical Abstract of
     the U.S.: 1970. 91st edition. Washington
     D.C., 1970.

U.S. Congress. Joint Economic Committee. Subcommit-
     tee on Federal Procurement and Regulation.
     Background Material on Economic Impact of Federal
     Procurement--1966. Washington, D.C.: Govern-
     ment Printing Office, 1966.

_____. Economic Aspects of Military Procurement
     and Supply. Report of the Subcommittee on De-
     fense Procurement. Washington, D.C.: Govern-
     ment Printing Office, 1960.

U.S. Congress. "Procurement Act." 84th Congress,
     2nd Sess. 1956. Title 10, U.S. Code.

U.S. Department of Defense. Defense Procurement
     Handbook. Washington, D.C.: Government Print-
     ing Office, 1965.

_____. "Five Year Trends in Defense Procurement,
     1958-1962." Convertibility of Space and Defense
     Resources to Civilian Needs: A Search for New
     Employment Potentials. Vol. II. Compiled for
     U.S. Senate, Subcommittee on Employment and Man-
     power of the Committee on Labor and Public Wel-
     fare. Washington, D.C.: Government Printing
     Office, 1964.

_____. Armed Services Procurement Regulations--
     1963 Edition. Washington, D.C.: U.S. Govern-
     ment Printing Office, 1963.

U.S. Department of Labor. Manpower Report of the
    President. Washington, D.C.: Government Print-
    ing Office, April, 1971.

                         OTHERS

Ault, John M.   "Establishing Meaningful Sales Goals
    Under Uncertain Market Conditions." American
    Marketing Association. Proceedings of the 48th
    National Conference. New York, 1965.

Kennedy, John J.   "Description and Analysis of the
    Organization of the Firm in the Defense Weapon
    Contract Industry." Unpublished Ph.D. disserta-
    tion, Ohio State University, 1962.

_____. "Practice and Theory in Negotiation: A
    Conceptual Model for Negotiation." American
    Marketing Association. Proceedings of the 48th
    National Conference. New York, 1965.

Loomba, R. P. Engineering Unemployment: Whose Re-
    sponsibility? San Jose, Calif.: San Jose State
    College, January 15, 1965.

Melman, Seymour, ed.   "Military Emphasis Blamed for
    State of the Economy." A Strategy for American
    Security. New York, April, 1963.

Mooney, Joseph D.   "Displaced Engineers and Scien-
    tists: An Analysis of the Labor Market Adjust-
    ment of Professional Personnel." Unpublished
    Ph.D. dissertation, Massachusetts Institute of
    Technology, 1965.

Sherman, Harold J.   "Marketing Organizations in the
    Defense/Space Industry." American Marketing
    Association. Proceedings of the 48th National
    Conference. New York, 1965.

Weidenbaum, Murray L.   "The Defense/Space Complex:
    Impact on Whom?" Challenge, April, 1965.

ABOUT THE AUTHORS

JOHN FRANCIS GORGOL was an expert in the new field of Management Science and served as Department Chairman, Management Department, University College at Rutgers, The State University, prior to his death. He worked in industry for a number of years before entering the teaching profession, thereby acquiring an insight into industry's workings, which helped in this writing.

Professor Gorgol was often called on to be guest speaker before many different professional societies. He was also Project Director for two research studies made for the state of New Jersey: "Anticipating Changes in Job Demand" and "The Impact of Numerically Controlled Production Equipment on Employment in New Jersey."

Mr. Gorgol had a B.A. and B.S. from Pennsylvania State University, and his M.A. and Ph.D from Columbia University. This writing was done under the guidance and encouragement of Dr. Seymour S. Melman of Columbia University.

IRA H. KLEINFELD is an Instructor in mathematics at the John Jay College of Criminal Justice. He has lectured in economics in the Mechanical Engineering Department at the City College of New York. Prior to this position, he was employed in the planning and development department of the Port of New York Authority.

Mr. Kleinfeld has received training as an economist and as an industrial engineer, having received his B.S. and M.S. degrees from the Department of Industrial and Management Engineering at Columbia University. He is currently completing his dissertation there for the Eng.Sc.D.